Moving On in Ministry

Moving On in Ministry

Discernment for Times of
Transition and Change

Edited by
Tim Ling

CHURCH HOUSE
PUBLISHING

Church House Publishing
Church House
Great Smith Street
London SW1P 3AZ

Published 2013 by Church House Publishing

ISBN 978 0 7151 4329 2

Typeset by Regent Typesetting, London
Printed in England by
CPI Group (UK) Ltd, Croydon CR0 4YY

Contents

Foreword   vii

Contributors   ix

Introduction   xi

 1 Approaching Transitions   1
   Tim Harle

 2 'Who shall I be?' Putting On Priesthood in the
   Church of England   17
   Amanda Bloor

 3 Growing into Responsibility   31
   Ian Aveyard

 4 Understanding and Enabling Clergy Careers   46
   Jane Sturges

 5 'Still in Saigon?' Ministry, Movies and Moving On   62
   Justin Lewis-Anthony

 6 A Pilgrimage to My Own Self? R. S. Thomas and
   the Poetic Character of Reflective Ministry   79
   Mark Pryce

 7 Body Building and Moving On with Liturgy   98
   Mark Beach

 8 From Parish to Chaplaincy   114
   Anthony Buckley

9　Letting Go and Holding On　　　　　　　　128
　　Viv Thomas

10　Affirmation and Accountability: Moving On
　　Through Ministerial Development Review　　142
　　Hazel Whitehead

11　Moving On in the 'Mixed-Economy Church'　156
　　Tim Ling

Foreword

The assumption that ministry is shared by both lay and ordained members of the church is now beyond being axiomatic. It is perhaps less well recognized that such a context of shared ministry requires significantly *more* rather than less support, education and development for clergy if they are to respond to the present requirements of the case. Indeed, it might be said that such specific provision for clergy is precisely a key to the advance we need in order to shape shared ministry in the transformed and transformative way which our present mission context requires.

The collection of essays in this book is accordingly very timely and welcome, precisely because it focuses on the experience of clergy in the midst of transition and change. Its emphasis on this perspective should not be misread as a case of clericalising the ministry. The partnership between all members of the church does not expunge their differences: it should instead allow each to flourish in their given vocation, and this book explores the experience of clergy in their calling now.

As a matter of policy in the Church of England resources for continuing ministerial development for clergy have been concentrated until recently on points of transition from one post to another. Without doubt, there is wisdom in this approach from both the practical and educational viewpoint. However, the experience of transition is not restricted to a physical move, as those whose ministries are essentially local know. Such is the current pace of change around the context of any ministry, whether a chaplaincy, a new form of church, a parish or a group of parishes, that to stay still is in effect to move. At a deeper level, even if we stay put physically, for the inner self there may be momentous transitions and changes every bit as dynamic as an event involving a removal van and a change of address.

The broad and generous approach of this book is therefore right on target in acknowledging the significance of all such transitions and the need for a response which is both reflective and practical. Its chapters bear witness in favour of the requirement to 'up our game' in providing diocesan support for clergy which helps them engage positively with change, for example through ministerial development review or professional guidance. Equally they represent the view that ministry is not merely a matter of policy and practical organisation but a divine vocation to a way of being grounded in the love of God. The transformation of ministry for mission in our present day requires that both of these perspectives are embraced and allowed to exercise their full influence on planning for ministerial support and development over the coming years.

I am pleased to commend this book for the stimulus it provides to all involved in the continuing development of clergy to think practically and creatively about the future of the church's ministry.

The Venerable Julian Hubbard

Contributors

Ian Aveyard is the former Director of Ordinands, Canterbury Diocese. He is author of the St John's Extension Study *God Thoughts*.

Mark Beach is the Dean of Rochester Cathedral, having previously served as Rugby Team Rector in the Coventry Diocese. He has recently completed a doctorate on the ecclesiology of the local church.

Anthony Buckley is Chaplain at Alleyn's School and Honorary Curate at St Barnabas, Dulwich. He is author of *At the Harbour Side: Considering Christianity* and the Grove booklet *Spirituality in Story.*

Amanda Bloor is Chaplain to the Bishop of Oxford. Her recently completed doctorate was on the topic of priestly vocation and involved a longitudinal study following men and women from their earliest days in theological training to their first parish.

Tim Harle is a Licensed Lay Minister (Reader) in the multi-parish benefice where he lives, Lay Canon at Bristol Cathedral and Visiting Fellow at Bristol Business School. He is Vice-Chair of MODEM, a network promoting mutual learning between churches and business in the areas of leadership, management and ministry, and author of *Embracing Chaos: Leadership Insights from Complexity Theory* (Grove Books, 2012).

Justin Lewis-Anthony is Rector of St Stephen's Church, Canterbury, and Associate Lecturer at the University of Kent. He is author of *If You Meet George Herbert on the Road, Kill Him* (Continuum, 2010). He has lectured and led retreats on film, popular culture and theology, and *pastoralia* across the country and in North America.

Tim Ling is the Church of England's National Adviser for Continuing Ministerial Development and the book's editor. He is author of *The Judaean Poor and the Fourth Gospel* (CUP, 2006) and co-editor of *Developing Faithful Ministers* (SCM Press, 2012).

Mark Pryce is adviser for Clergy Continuing Ministerial Education in the Diocese of Birmingham. His publications include: *Finding a Voice: Men, Women and the Community of the Church* (SCM Press, 1996), *A Literary Companion to the Lectionary* (SPCK, 2001) and *A Literary Companion for Festivals* (SPCK, 2003).

Jane Sturges is a Senior Lecturer in Organizational Behaviour in the Department of Management at King's College London. She is a member of the editorial boards of *Journal of Organizational Behavior* and *International Journal of Work, Organisation and Emotion*.

Viv Thomas is the Director of Formation and Honorary Teaching Pastor at St Paul's Hammersmith. He is the author of *Future Leader*, *Second Choice*, *Paper Boys* and *The Spectacular Ordinary Life*. He speaks and teaches in churches and conferences around the United Kingdom and the world. He is an Associate Lecturer at Spurgeon's College and lectures at other similar institutions.

Hazel Whitehead is the Director of Discipleship, Vocation and Ministry for the Diocese of Guildford and Co-Chair of the South Central Regional Training Partnership. Her recent DMin. thesis was an attempt to provide a theological and biblical rationale for Ministerial Development Review.

Introduction

The human mind may devise many plans, but it is the purpose of the LORD that will be established.

Proverbs 19.21

As the final touches to this book were being made, a President of the United States was re-elected, the 105th Archbishop of Canterbury was announced, and the Director General of the BBC resigned amid controversy. The transitions that are currently taking place in their lives and the communities they represent will very rapidly become eclipsed by other events. Change happens. Sometimes it's contested and sometimes it appears to be planned, occasionally it is thrust upon us. The essays in this book are intended to support theological reflection around the changes we face in our lives and more specifically around transitions in ministry. While these changes won't necessarily be taking place in the full gaze of the global media they will be significant and potentially disturbing – pregnant with potential. It has therefore been the Church of England's espoused policy since *The Continuing Education of the Church's Ministers* (GS Misc 122, 1980) to focus its continuing ministerial education and development provision around transitions in ministry. There are sound reasons for this policy. However, there is also a danger, unless we are mindful, that it may lead to the assumption we are able to manage change with tidy developmental interventions. This book will not provide you with instructions on change management or leadership technique. Rather, in its 11 chapters, I hope that it will contribute to our mindfulness around change by describing, exploring and questioning our experiences of transition and the range of theological resources that we draw upon to enable us to faithfully attend to 'the purpose of the Lord'.

The closest that the book gets to a change management model is in its opening chapter in which Tim Harle offers a critical reflection on the 'S-curve' as a framework for approaching transitions. He uses the model to challenge us to reflect on how we locate ourselves in change, our understanding of God and divine action, and calls us to explore our capacity and resources for living comfortably out of control.

The following three chapters are the fruit of research projects that have sought to listen to the voices of clergy at various stages in ministry. Amanda Bloor explores what it means to become a priest. Ian Aveyard focuses particularly on the transition into incumbency, and Jane Sturges describes how clergy perceptions of career success develop throughout ministry. A common element in each of their essays is the idea of 'being a good priest' and the struggle to shape a sustainable ministerial identity. Amanda reflects that the questions, 'Who shall I be?' and 'What shall I do?' are crucial elements of the transition to ordained ministry. Ian echoes her concern that the answer must be more than the assumption of 'an imagined (and sometimes imaginary) idealized identity'. These at times, he argues, function as controlling narratives that have the potential to disable us from attending to our present call and the summons to the much wider prospect – 'taking our part in the fullness of ministry in God's Church'. Jane, writing from the perspective of an Organizational Psychologist, reflects back to the Church how, amidst the apparently conflicting interests of calling and career, clergy present some distinctive notions of career success rooted in the calling to priesthood.

The language of transitions suggests movement. When we add the words 'career' and 'developments' we are periodically faced with a feeling of absence, that we are neither developing nor possessing a career. Tim Harle, when he describes the 'S-curve', importantly raises questions about how we conceive of growth and decline. But what place might there be for despondency – the sin of *accidia* that can particularly affect those whose lives are focused on love and service? This is the theme of Justin Lewis-Anthony's chapter which meditates on two films, *The Way* and

Of Gods and Men, and exposes us to the condition of being trapped and not realizing it, and of being trapped and realizing it. By seeing the world reflected in cinematic art and helping us to understand how that reflection works, he both reassures and challenges us to attend to our vocation. Mark Pryce's following essay takes us from the cinema to the poetry and autobiography of R. S. Thomas and the wisdom he distils in his reflections on times of transition from one phase of ministry to another. Mark argues that R. S. Thomas's reflective approach to ministry enabled him to both trace his journey and to construct a sense of meaning out of his experiences, to capture for a moment the 'complex, contradictory, fleeting and recurring material of self-in-relation to God and the mystery of God disclosed or hidden in others'. He advocates such reflections as a discipline for clergy to consider.

Mark Beach starts his essay by reflecting on his theological understanding of the place of the minister in the life of the Church – that his leadership is to be 'formed and lived out in the whole Church, not just in its ordained leadership'. He attends to the disturbance that this causes and explores the implications of his own thinking on our liturgical practices and makes an impassioned plea that our worship should adequately describe the nature of the worshipping community – the Body of Christ. Anthony Buckley continues by also reflecting on the place of the minister in the life of the Church, questioning the place of the chaplain in a parochial world. He describes the experience of the move from parish to chaplaincy and the feeling of no longer being 'one of us' and offers counsel to watch over one's spiritual life, learn from desert life and to enjoy incarnational life. He concludes with a lover's excitement telling the story of two new young vocations.

The next two chapters make a specific appeal for space to attend to the themes of imagined identities, vocation and transition: Viv Thomas, through mentoring, and Hazel Whitehead, through Ministerial Development Review. They both look to Scripture for a theological underpinning of their practice. Viv uses the stories of Jesus at Nazareth (Mark 6.1–6) and Peter and Cornelius (Acts 10) to reflect on what is required to equip people in the dual role of letting go and holding on, disavowing unbelief and being open to the voice of God. Hazel also works with two texts, Exodus 18 and Revelation 2—3. She draws out three themes: the complexity of vocation, the importance of place and the nature of the human condition. She concludes by underlining the importance of being 'open to God's nudge, love and admonition'.

The book concludes with a chapter reflecting on our current context of a 'mixed-economy church'. It uses the episode of Paul's visit to Jerusalem (Acts 15/Galatians 2) as a lens through which to explore our more institutional understandings of change and our place within them. It uses the metaphors of revisiting Jerusalem, remembering the poor, and realizing our poverty, to help us to think about our particular hopes and anxieties, the boundaries of our communities and the authorities that we privilege as we move on in ministry.

I am very grateful to the contributors for the care with which they have wrestled with the brief to reflect theologically on transitions in ministry. I am struck by the common threads that emerged in the process of writing of travelling with our memories, real and imagined, and the call to mindfulness. I hope that through describing, exploring and questioning our experiences of transition and by pointing to some theological resources you will find some helpful companions for your journey.

Tim Ling
November 2012

I

Approaching Transitions

TIM HARLE

'Can you live with what you've delivered?' The Managing Director's question could only be answered in one way if I expected my career to develop at the company where I had just completed three tough years at the head of a corporate change programme. The elation of delivering on time, if slightly over budget and not quite complete, was followed by a refreshing family holiday. It was my first day back at work when I was invited to the MD's office. Later that morning, I forsook my corner office and PA – and my place in the company's organization chart – to drive down the M4 to a new, undefined, role. The months and years that followed were to prove the most hellish, and ultimately most satisfying, of my working life.

Our consideration of transitions begins by introducing a framework for change, S-curves, based on observations in the natural world. It examines different attitudes to change, then moves on to look at continuous and discontinuous transitions, and what might trigger them. A consideration of individual and organizational transitions leads to a focus on the transitional, or liminal, space between S-curves. This raises questions about the extent to which we can control our situation, and highlights our differing needs for security in times of uncertainty. The chapter concludes by considering some implications for the minister, who may be moving on.

Introducing S-curves

If a well-meaning consultant had told me, as I struggled to come to terms with my new company role, that I had just tipped off the top of one S-curve and was in the maelstrom trying to get a foot on a new one, I might well have decked them. Yet now, with the benefit of hindsight and an accumulation of community wisdom, I recognize that is what was going on. Would it have helped if I had known such a framework in advance? Possibly. Would it have made the transition any less painful? Probably not. Yet we only have to look at the natural world to see such patterns all around us. The rhythm of the seasons – spring, summer, autumn, winter – can be expressed in the shape of an 'S': slow initial growth, blossoming and healthy development, followed by slow decline, even death. We see such curves of growth and decay not only in our lives, but in history, from civilizations to companies and churches.

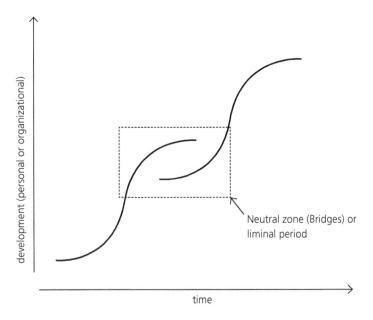

Figure 1. S-curves of growth and decay

In my experience, the S-curve framework is hugely helpful to many people, including ministers from different denominations, and we will use it in this chapter. But we need to note three aspects, which need to be drawn out in the context of transitions.

First, S-curves can encourage a view of growth being considered as good in itself. As current debates about the economy and the very future of our planet show, there are profound questions to address. We need to be careful about how we consider growth: growth in depth, in understanding, in community, in relationships, may be more significant – and satisfying – than growth according to traditional measures.

Second, S-curves may encourage a linear approach to time. The idea of *kairos* time, a moment to be embraced, may well be more helpful in the context of a transition than *chronos* time, measured by our clocks and calendars.

Lastly, there is the question of where to focus our attention. As we will see below, and as my opening example demonstrated, we often concentrate on the period between the top of one curve and the bottom of another. A perspective that encourages natural growth should celebrate the continuing transitions that occur within an S-curve.

Learning from nature

In the natural world, transitions are a sign of health. They may involve slow, even hidden, growth. They may involve more obvious transformation, as in a caterpillar to a butterfly. They often involve growing pains. Yet they are wondrous. The perspective of this chapter is that transitions are entirely natural, and should be embraced. It seeks to weave together the warp of the organizational ecologist with the weft of the practical theologian.

I once met a bishop who asked what my work involved. 'I work with people going through change', I replied. The bishop paused for a moment of episcopal reflection before responding, 'Ah, change and decay.' Whatever the pastoral benefits of the hymn, 'Abide with me', H. F. Lyte's inclusion of the line 'change and decay in all around I see' was hardly felicitous. For many people, change has negative connotations. And yet change is going on all the time, whether we realize it or not. As Cardinal Newman wrote, 'To live is to change.'

Our attitude to what we see as unchangeable was brought home to me by a member of a group I was working with. To illustrate an image of changelessness, I shared a picture of a local rural parish church with its solid tower. This person, who knew far more than me about ecclesiastical architecture, pointed out a fifteenth-century original, with additions up to the Victorian era. What we think of as unchanging has, in fact, changed. We see something similar reflected in the growing interest in more dynamic perspectives of God, such as a view of the Holy Trinity characterized by mutual indwelling, where images such as dance are applied in reaction to earlier, more static, models.[1]

Another lesson from nature is that disturbance is vital for health. This is encapsulated in the Benedictine vow of conversion of life, beautifully described by a former abbot of Ampleforth as 'a vow to change, to never remain still either in self-satisfied fulfilment or self-denying despair'.[2] Rosie Ward highlights the point at an institutional level: 'In an Anglican context (and it's the same for most of the denominations), unless we change, we will die. We face the choice between a comfortable death – if that is not a contradiction in terms – and an uncomfortable life.'[3] We will consider the importance of healthy disturbance, and the implications for our security, later in the chapter.

I wonder how much time executive coaches, counsellors and spiritual directors spend on transitions that have become a crisis. Words written about organizational change draw attention to the possibility of avoiding a crisis by embracing an attitude of renewal: 'Enormous managerial energy... [has] been devoted to turnarounds, rescues, and massive "change" programs, yet isn't the real goal to avoid a crisis-sized transformation problem by creating a capacity for continuous renewal deep within the company?'[4] A 'capacity for continuous renewal deep within' (ourselves ... our churches ...) resonates with the Christian gospel and provides us with an opportunity for considering life's transitions, whether they are ongoing or take the form of one-off changes.

Continuous and discontinuous change

Saul's experience on the road to Damascus may be the exception
to prove a rule. An understanding of evangelism in process terms
accords with a view of continuous transitions. The Hebrew and
Christian Scriptures offer us examples of both continuous and
discontinuous change. The Exodus and Exile were epic national
events, where a return to a previous life was not possible. 'By the
waters of Babylon there is no way back to the old Jerusalem.'[5]
Paul's writings offer examples of discontinuity: 'If anyone is in
Christ, there is a new creation: everything old has passed away;
see, everything has become new!' (2 Cor. 5.17). In contrast, the
Book of Revelation offers a vision where renewal is continuous:
'The one who was seated on the throne said, "See, I am making
all things new"' (Rev. 21.5). The Hebrew understanding of the
breath of God also offers a picture of ongoing renewal: 'When
you send forth your spirit, they are created, and you renew the
face of the earth' (Ps. 104.32).

Kurt Lewin contributed a great deal to the discipline of social
psychology. But I am not sure his 'unfreeze-change-refreeze'
model, and especially subsequent simplistic applications of it, are
helpful. They emphasize the idea that change is something that
happens between periods of stability, and that it can be controlled.
Instead, we need an approach that helps us to understand both
the continuing nature of change, and the fact that it can rarely be
controlled. 'Change management' is one of the great oxymorons
of our time, and complexity theory is helping us understand the
implications of this.

If there is one discipline that has transformed my attitude to
change in the past decade, it is the amalgam of scientific discoveries popularly known as chaos, or complexity, theory.[6] Some of
its language has entered our popular vocabulary – people speak
of 'tipping points' without necessarily understanding non-linear
equations. And the 'butterfly effect' reminds us that small changes
in initial conditions can have a mighty impact. The implications
for our planning and strategies can be profound: 'strategy may
emerge inadvertently and unintentionally from socialized practices engaged in by people who do not identify themselves as

strategists'.[7] This leads us to consider how a transition might begin: deliberately or accidentally, planned or unplanned.

Triggers for transition

How do we move along and between S-curves? On many occasions, I have been struck by the deep insights revealed by asking people to draw a period of change they have encountered in S-curve form. From beautifully appointed offices in the City of London via Miners' Welfare Clubs to church groups, the drawings often reveal aspects of which even close colleagues are unaware. A large blank space represented a hitherto unknown period in intensive care, where personal attitudes to life and others were transformed. On another occasion, the expert from head office crafted a beautiful series of perfectly shaped curves. 'There's not much sign of disturbance there', came the comment from the hard-pressed worker on the front line.

One crucial question to consider is whether transitions are triggered externally, or from within. Any answer is likely to include elements of both, and refer both to our personalities and the environments in which we find ourselves. Edwin Friedman's experience as a rabbi and family therapist enables him to warn against simplistic either/or answers to such a question: 'It is often said that new ways of seeing or cohering things must originate from outside of a system. My experience with families and institutions, however, is that truly novel concepts can begin from within, provided someone can get "outside" of its emotional processes while remaining physically inside.'[8]

This enables us to see different triggers for transition. They may be planned, such as moving through the education system from primary to secondary (and perhaps tertiary) education. Or they may be the result of a disruptive event: losing a job, illness, bereavement. They may be the result of an external stimulus, such as an invitation or suggestion from a trusted adviser. Or they may result from something internal: a desire for growth, a growing sense of dissatisfaction.

Such considerations may be summed up using words whose

familiarity may dull our appreciation of them: vocation or calling. Scripture can support advocates of contrasting approaches to calling: the external and the internal. Moses was confronted by the burning bush (Ex. 3.1–6), while Elijah heard (sic) God not in the wind, earthquake or fire, but in 'a sound of sheer silence' (1 Kings 19.11–13). The experience of the disciples on the Emmaus road offers an interesting example of both external and internal triggers: 'Were not our hearts burning within us?' (Luke 24.32).

The respected management writers Warren Bennis and Bill George have both applied the image of a crucible to formative moments which affect people's outlook and attitudes.[9] Those who know Hebrew scripture may well be reminded of the image of a refiner's fire (Mal. 3.3). Our different spiritualities, and psychological and social preferences, may also affect our attitude to transitions. Once again, I find the Benedictine tradition a great help, especially the living tension between stability and conversion of life. The Benedictine approach also encourages us in our next consideration: the role of the individual and the community of which they are part.

Personal and organizational transitions

Edwin Friedman draws attention to an important shift in perspective that is relevant both to individualized churches and atomized introvert ministers. 'The quantum jump forward was provided by the pioneers in the family therapy movement who began to focus on relationship processes rather than discrete personalities.'[10] The main focus of this book is on personal transitions. But it is vital to understand that the framework we are considering operates at many levels, from the individual via the team to the organization and beyond. We saw that S-curves can be applied at many levels, from individuals to civilizations. Such repeating patterns at different levels bring to mind the concept of fractals, echoing repeating patterns in such natural features as coastlines.

'Where is your church on its S-curve?' This discussion starter invariably generates animated, and ultimately constructive, conversations. What church are we considering? From a perspective

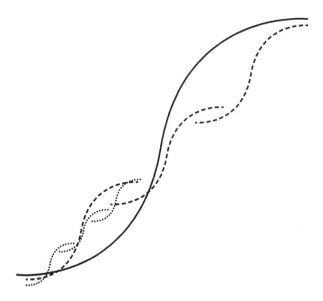

Figure 2. S-curves are fractal, showing a repeating pattern at many levels

of the Great Schism and Reformation, the church is quite a long way along its curve. From the perspective of the newly planted daughter church, fresh expression or eco-congregation, it is somewhere quite near the beginning. Both answers are equally valid. And where is the minister on their S-curve(s)? Length in post, biological age and relationships have their part to play, but more subtle attitudes may be at work. Linked with the individual and the church may be one or more teams, each with, literally, a life of its own. Understanding these different rhythms – especially mismatches between individual and organizational S-curves – can be invaluable in helping to deal with energy-sapping tensions at times of transition.

As with Elisabeth Kübler-Ross's work on grief, it is vital not to reduce our approach to a linear one, with transitional stages to be worked through sequentially. We can also mention James Fowler's work on stages of faith, which has been critiqued by Nicola Slee from a feminist, less linear perspective.[11] We currently see expectations of less ordered phases in life from a number of different directions, from the postmodern project to the expectations of Generation Y. Growing demands for less traditional work and career patterns challenge inherited paternalist attitudes,[12] a trend we see in churches as well as business.[13]

Whether approached in a linear fashion or not, transitions often involve passing through a period of uncertainty. It is to this aspect we now turn.

Transitional space

The best-known approach to transitions is probably that of William Bridges. He has highlighted the significance of a 'neutral zone' between a period characterized by ending, losing and letting go, and a period of new beginnings. Writing in the preface to the 25th anniversary edition of his pioneering book, Bridges emphasizes what is distinctive about a transition: 'Without a transition, a change is just a rearrangement of the furniture.' More profoundly he notes how, after publication of his book, 'there were hundreds of thousands of people out there who were trying to make sense out of transition, but far fewer who wanted to be in the business of facilitating death and rebirth'.[14]

Anthropologists can help our appreciation of the neutral zone, especially through the notion of liminal space. Once again, we see examples operating at different levels, from national to personal. The wilderness wanderings recorded in Exodus can be viewed as a liminal period between slavery in Egypt and freedom in the Promised Land. And Jesus' life includes significant periods of liminality: from the temptations in the wilderness, which preceded his public ministry, to the Garden of Gethsemane 'on the night before he died'. Alan Roxburgh's words referring to a group can also be applied to the individual: 'the liminal group is in an unstructured state. Old rules no longer apply; they simply will not work. Because of this fact, liminality becomes a place of undefined potential. Something new can be discovered.'[15] Roxburgh notes the importance of listening to voices from the edge,[16] a perspective which resonates with Penny Jamieson's personal and theological reflections.[17]

The Dutch organizational ecologist Peter Robertson deploys the powerful image of the salmon leap as a metaphor for the period of turbulence between S-curves.[18] The salmon uses the turbulence of cascading water to climb waterfalls when returning to spawning grounds. Yet this point of great opportunity is also a point of great danger, as Canadian brown bears looking for food can testify. Such a powerful image can have unexpected lessons for transitions, as I discovered at our local supermarket.

'I just want to thank you for how you helped me.' My weekly shop was interrupted by a fellow shopper. I must have looked blank, for my companion continued, 'The washing machine did it for me.' I made a wild, but correct, guess at the connection. This person, a specialist in their field, had taken part in a workshop I had led, and had remembered the turbulent water of the salmon leap in terms of being trapped in the rotating drum of a washing machine. Understanding they had reached the top of one S-curve, the image had given them the courage to seek a new S-curve: a new challenge which had personal and professional benefits both for the individual and their co-workers.

Mention of turbulence leads us to reflect on a crucial theological point, which underlies many of our social and psychological approaches to transitions. It concerns the question of chaos and control.

On being comfortably out of control

A traditional Western understanding of chaos is that it is something to be avoided, or at least controlled. Robin Greenwood and Hugh Burgess note how Christian theology 'became associated with a simplistic form of Hellenistic dualism, rooted in the changeless, unmoved eternity of God and the unchangeable mess of the material world. Our inheritance is the traditional, stable Christian understanding of creation and salvation history, loathing heretical chaos and travelling from a simple beginning to its ultimate goal.'[19] We see examples of attempted control in any number of rules and regulations, and we sometimes see it in people's attempts to control their own lives. A complexity perspective offers radically new insights on control, which impinge on two of the mightiest theological concepts of all.

First, the creation. Instead of a traditional reading of Genesis 1 with God moving and separating to control the primeval chaos, Catherine Keller offers a wonderful new perspective. 'If Elohim does not, contrary to most readings, unilaterally order a world into existence, Elohim *"lets be"*.'[20] A modern example is offered by the internet giant, CISCO. To encourage more international and cross-functional innovation, they promoted the idea of 'Let it happen!' in contrast to the more usual 'Make it happen!' slogan.

The second great theological theme we can revisit is the incarnation. Whether in the Lucan narrative beloved of nativity plays, or the Johannine Word becoming flesh, we see a transition on an almost unimaginable scale. Kester Brewin's startling Christology lays down a challenge. 'Becoming incarnate will mean the same for us as it did for Christ. We will have to experience being small and defenceless, requiring nurture from our host-world just as Christ needed Mary's milk ... like Christ we must take this risk of interdependence, this risk of being born, this risk of life.'[21] Note the significant roles played both by the individual and the environment.

Meg Wheatley links the natural world to our fear of chaos. Her words addressed to leaders can apply not only to their community, but their own lives. 'Life is cyclical – we pass through different moods; we live through seasons; we have times of rich harvests and times of bleak winter. Life uses cycles to create newness. We move from the old to the new only if we let go. Instead of fleeing from the fearful place of chaos or trying to rescue people from it, leaders can help people stay with the chaos, help them walk through it together, and look for the new insights and capacities that always emerge.'[22]

Some of the most exciting developments in contemporary thinking about churches and ministry come from the Emergent Village community.[23] Their approach is captured by the subtitle of Tim Keel's book: Embracing a paradigm of narrative, metaphor and chaos. 'What if leaders and communities resisted the impulse to assert and gain control over their environment when it begins to get a little funky and disruptive? What if leaders sought to stay present in the midst of chaos in order to discern the presence and activity of the Holy Spirit hovering in love and creativity over a new act of creation?'[24]

Talk of turbulence, neutral zones and being out of control raises questions about our need for security. A helpful psychological perspective is provided by Attachment Theory, which we now consider.

Finding a secure base

Two related concepts are important when considering transitions: attachment and exploration. John Bowlby and Mary Ainsworth observed how children treated attachment figures, such as parents and caregivers, as a secure base from which to explore. Attachment is now recognized more widely in adulthood: for example, Kohlrieser et al[25] apply the secure base to relationships between leaders and followers. Robertson[26] expanded the concept by introducing matter attachment: instead of finding security in a person, some prefer a non-personal object of attachment.

As anyone who has suggested even the gentlest change in church order can testify, we find security in a number of things. When the possibility of them being changed is raised, some feel anxious. Lest anyone think this is confined to a favourite pew or the *Book of Common Prayer*, consider the significance to some of a data projector or drum kit. A more complex example of attachment applies to – possibly idealized – notions of priesthood. If churches are being reorganized into larger groupings, the minister will need to consider whether they see themselves, and are being treated by others, as a secure base as a person or on account of their priestly or ministerial role. The former perspective tends to people attachment, the latter to matter.

During a transition, someone strong on people attachment may find it difficult to disentangle personal relationships from external events. And researchers are beginning to ask what we can learn from perceiving God as a secure base, an area I trust will be theologically and pastorally fruitful.[27]

Attachment is not an either/or preference, as in the unfortunate labels often used in the context of the MBTI® indicator, so beloved of clergy: we are all somewhere on a spectrum between people and matter attachment.[28] That is something to recognize and celebrate.

Once we are securely attached, we can begin our exploration. Arising from our evolutionary heritage, we all have a tendency to explore, though this varies. Once again, our preference is somewhere on a spectrum between preferring stability or relentless exploration. Anyone can explore: people with a tendency to matter attachment can be highly innovative. The key point for the minister, both in relation to their personal life and as a potential point of attachment for others, is to recognize different secure bases.

How does a secure base emerge? Studies with people and matter attachment highlight the importance of consistency. Consistency encourages a secure base, and a secure base gives us a point from which to explore. Such consistency should be seen between small everyday encounters and grand gestures. Once again, we see fractals at play.[29] Amy Edmondson's work observing teams, especially in high-pressure environments such as hospitals, has identified a similar idea: zones of psychological safety, within which questions and concerns can be raised, and learning developed.[30]

As part of security in transitions, trust is vital. And trust develops, not through grand pronouncements, but through the relentless consistency experienced in everyday interactions. Kieran Sweeney cites a telling example from the fraught world of interdisciplinary work in health and social care. 'Trust arose from the conversations … whose patterns co-created the system's self-organisation … encouraged by the monthly meetings and weekly updates. From this perspective, trust became an emergent property of the system. In turn, the trust fed back, positively and iteratively.'[31] Three points arise from this example. First, there was a mixture of self-organization (conversations) and structure (monthly meetings, weekly updates). Second, trust is properly described as an emergent property: it cannot be imposed. Third, feedback is vital: we need to learn to observe, listen and act.

This practical example of trust concludes our initial consideration of transitions. It remains to summarize some practical implications.

Implications for the minister

Further chapters will explore implications of transitions in particular contexts. Here we can note some scene-setting ideas.

The first is a theological one. As Stephen Pickard has noted, our approach to ministry reflects our understanding of God: 'a collaborative theory of ministry is inherent in the character of the triune God present in creation and redemption'.[32] Our attitudes to change and transitions are likely to reflect our understanding of God and divine action.

Second, observations from the world around us show that transitions are a sign of health, even if they may involve some disturbance. There is a growing interest in applying organic, non-linear approaches to church communities. Although written for a Christian audience, I was encouraged to learn[33] that Joseph Myers' work[34] has helped a county council in the UK.

Next, we need to be alert to internal and external triggers for change. We can do no better than follow the multi-sensory example of Habakkuk: 'I will keep watch to see what he will say to me' (Hab. 2.1).

Fourth, ministers may find their home at different stages of an S-curve. Fresh insights from Ephesians 4 have come from the missiologists Michael Frost and Alan Hirsch. They draw together the works of apostles, prophets, evangelists, pastors and teachers into the APEPT framework.[35] Their plea is for churches to understand the disturbing need for apostles and prophets to avoid the reassuring ossification that sets in with pastors and teachers. Andrew Gear has helpfully mapped these roles onto organizational life cycles.[36]

Lastly, whether we prefer the language of the neutral zone or liminal space, we need to be aware of our differing preferences for security and exploration as we proceed through periods of uncertainty.

Notes

1. Stephen Pickard, *Theological Foundations for Collaborative Ministry*, Farnham: Ashgate, 2009, p. 4; Ali Green, *A Priesthood of Both Sexes*, London: SPCK, 2011, pp. 89–92.

2. Timothy Wright OSB in Kit Dollard, Anthony Marett-Crosby and Timothy Wright, *Doing Business with Benedict*, London: Continuum, 2002, p. 201.

3. Rosie Ward, *Growing Women Leaders*, Abingdon: BRF, 2008, p. 170.

4. Gary Hamel and C. K. Prahalad, *Competing for the Future*, new edn, Boston MA: Harvard Business School Press, 1996, p. x.

5. Alan J. Roxburgh, *The Missionary Congregation, Leadership, and Liminality*, Harrisburg PA: Trinity Press International, 1997, p. 57.

6. Tim Harle, *Embracing Chaos*, Cambridge: Grove Books, 2011.

7. Robert C. H. Chia and Robin Holt, *Strategy without Design*, Cambridge: Cambridge University Press, 2009, pp. 122f.

8. Edwin H. Friedman, *A Failure of Nerve*, New York NY: Seabury, 2007, p. 130.

9. Warren G. Bennis and Robert J. Thomas, *Geeks and Geezers*, Boston MA: Harvard Business School Press, 2002; Bill George, *True North*, San Francisco CA: Jossey-Bass, 2007.

10. Friedman, *A Failure of Nerve*, p. 127.

11. Nicola Slee, *Women's Faith Development*, Aldershot: Ashgate, 2004; cf. James W. Fowler, *Becoming Adult, Becoming Christian*, San Francisco CA: Jossey-Bass, 2000.

12. Amanda Sinclair, *Leadership for the Disillusioned*, Crows Nest NSW: Allen & Unwin, 2007; Averil Leimon, François Moscovici and Helen Goodier, *Coaching Women to Lead*, Hove: Routledge, 2011.

13. Barbara Brown Taylor, *Leaving Church*, New York NY: HarperSanFrancisco, 2006; Ronni Lamont, *Leaping the Vicarage Wall*, London: Continuum, 2011.

14. William Bridges, *Transitions*, 2nd edn, Cambridge MA: Da Capo, 2004, p. xii.

15. Roxburgh, *The Missionary Congregation*, p. 32.

16. Roxburgh, *The Missionary Congregation*, p. 57.

17. Penny Jamieson, *Living at the Edge*, London: Mowbray, 1997.

18. Peter Robertson, *Always Change a Winning Team*, London: Cyan, 2005, p. 126.

19. Robin Greenwood and Hugh Burgess, *Power*, London: SPCK, 2005, p. 56.

20. Catherine Keller, *Face of the Deep*, Abingdon: Routledge, 2003, p. 195, italics original.

21. Kester Brewin, *The Complex Christ*, London: SPCK, 2004, p. 52.

22. Margaret J. Wheatley, *Finding Our Way*, San Francisco CA: Berrett-Koehler, 2005, p. 127.

23. See www.emergentvillage.org.

24. Tim Keel, *Intuitive Leadership*, Grand Rapids MI: Baker, 2007, p. 240.

25. George Kohlrieser, Susan Goldsworthy and Duncan Coombe, *Care to Dare*, San Francisco CA, Jossey-Bass, 2012.

26. Robertson, *Always Change a Winning Team*.

27. Pehr Granqvist and Lee A. Kirkpatrick, 'Attachment and Religious Representations and Behavior', in Jude Cassidy and Phillip R. Shaver (eds), *Handbook of Attachment*, 2nd edn, New York NY: Guilford, 2008, pp. 906–933, p. 911.

28. For further information on attachment and exploration, see http://www.human-insight.com/tools-techniques-and-learning/aem-cube.php.

29. Tim Harle, 'Fractal Leadership', in JoAnn Danelo Barbour and Gill Robinson Hickman (eds), *Leadership for Transformation*, San Francisco CA: Jossey-Bass, 2011b, pp. 33–49.

30. Amy Edmondson, *Teaming*, San Francisco CA: Jossey-Bass, 2012, pp. 115–148.

31. Kieran Sweeney, *Complexity in Primary Care*, Abingdon: Radcliffe, 2006, pp. 87f.

32. Pickard, *Theological Foundations for Collaborative Ministry*, p. 153.

33. From Esther Ridsdale's presentation, 'Enabling a Flourishing Civil Society', at the MODEM conference, *Leading Across Boundaries*. See http://www.modem-uk.org/conference2011.html. Myers is part of the Emergent Village community (see n. 23).

34. Joseph R. Myers, *Organic Community*, Grand Rapids MI: Baker, 2007.

35. Michael Frost and Alan Hirsch, *The Shaping of Things to Come*, Peabody MA: Hendrickson, 2003.

36. In an unpublished Diocese of Oxford paper, 'The Shape of Things to Come'. I am grateful to my colleague, Keith Lamdin, for drawing attention to Gear's work linking the APEPT framework and organizational life cycles.

2

'Who shall I be?' Putting On Priesthood in the Church of England

AMANDA BLOOR

In 2005, *Country Life* magazine illustrated its search for 'Britain's best-loved parson' with a photograph of a neatly bearded priest, in pale linen jacket, clerical collar and panama hat, cycling majestically towards a tidily kept country church.[1] In the same year, *The Times Magazine* celebrated the ministry of ordained women with a front cover showing a young priest conducting all-age worship and sharing her pulpit with a soft toy.[2] Although media ciphers, both images reflect something important about public perceptions of ordained ministry, and about the models that shape the possibilities of those investigating vocations to priesthood. Becoming a priest is not just a simple matter of responding to God's calling, or of recognizing gifts that can be offered in service to the Church. It also involves the negotiation of complex issues of public representation typified by the two extremes described above. Clergy are required to identify and prioritize the supernatural 'calling' of God but submit to the discernment and authority of the Church, and are commonly required to respond to the needs and wishes of their local communities and congregations while maintaining a clear institutional identity and obedience to those ordained to Episcopal leadership. Anglican priesthood is at the same time deeply personal and irreducibly corporate; it is shaped by context but subject ultimately only to God. Little wonder that new entrants to the 'clerical profession' find themselves challenged by questions of authority, identity, ambiguity and practice.

Anthropology suggests that religion combines two seemingly divergent concepts: meaning is found through cultural practices (in Christianity, for example, through such things as ritual, shared belief, biblical interpretation and sacramental actions) and through recognizing the power and authority of the religious structure itself (in the Church of England, demonstrated by the disciplinary, pastoral and teaching role of bishops, synodical government and Establishment).[3] Christianity adds a third element to this paradox, that of the personal intervention of the Holy Spirit. So an individual believing in a calling to ordained ministry has somehow to combine being part of a worshipping, faithful community of believers, being subject to the authority of the institution of the Church (and also being prepared to represent that authority to others) and being ultimately accountable and continually responsive to God. The transition from being a member of the laity, no matter how heavily involved with local expressions of church, to being ordained and licensed by the bishop, requires not only the acquisition of particular practical and theoretical skills, but also the ability to find a congruence between one's personal identity, forged over a lifetime, and the imposed identity of priest in the Church of England, with all the assumptions of privilege, eccentricity and increasing irrelevance that this may imply.[4]

Current literature about priesthood in the Church of England seems reluctant to be too specific about the nature of the calling in contemporary contexts. Books written by bishops (who are considered by virtue of their calling to have particular insight into what it is to be a parish priest) and other senior clergy about the theological and practical elements of priesthood, are often based upon individual understandings, representative personal experiences or typical pastoral situations. They can provide examples of inspirational practice, but do not always provide relevant, realistic or helpful models of ordained ministry. Texts telling autobiographical stories of priesthood, often to illustrate the experiences of a discrete group (such as the first tranche of ordained women), or to describe those with particularly sacrificial or eccentric ministries, can be entertaining or enlightening to read, but their specificity leaves them less than helpful to individuals who do not fit the models of the clergy they describe. Some studies investigate ecclesiological, psychological, pastoral, ethical, historical or theological aspects of priesthood, but because of their academic detachment, do not provide easy ways of combining their discoveries with lived experience. Turning to the available literature does not seem to provide individuals who believe that they have a vocation to ordained ministry with adequate information about what it could mean to them to become a priest.

How then do men and women, believing that they are called to ordained ministry in the Church of England, assess what it might mean for them to 'put on' priesthood? A long-term research project[5] revealed that many of them measured their vocation not against theory or theology, but against the example of priests whom they had known and admired. Instead of having a clear doctrinal, theological or institutional understanding of what twenty-first-century Anglican priesthood demands, they looked back to idealized visions that offered only partial images of lived ministries, and expected that they would themselves live out their callings in similar circumstances. For those who were excited about their vocation, this could lead to unrealistic expectations of the ways in which they would approach training and their future deployment by the Church. Paul,[6] for example, inspired by the example of a public evangelist who had nurtured his faith, described priesthood as 'the most noble, exotic, wild' calling imaginable; an ambition that was 'probably the most dangerous thing I've ever done'. He wanted to 'fight for the Church of England, fight for evangelism, fight for the things this country needs', and when asked where he saw his future ministry, replied, 'I'd like to be a bishop!' adding hastily, 'that was a joke.' Paul's initial vision of his future ministry included running a large church that was 'heavily involved with evangelism' and social outreach, and working with some major figures from the evangelical wing of the Church of England.

Judith, in contrast, had family members who had served the Church in various types of ministry, and described being depressed by a visit to a retired missionary living in very reduced circumstances. She thought of her vocation as 'grim', was dismissive of the low stipend offered to priests and 'wished that God had called someone else'. With conservative views on women and headship, she insisted that she would have to work within a team setting under the leadership of a male priest, hoping to find a colleague who was 'wise and Godly and respectable'. Like other ordinands whose vocations were reluctantly accepted rather than eagerly met, she saw her future ministry as a time of struggle and duty rather than of joyful fulfilment, but like her more idealistic contemporaries, based her expectations upon the 'ideal' ministries of which she had previous experience. Nick, who came from a family where generations had served as priests, had reservations about his ability to live up to the standard set by his ancestors in ministry and the belief that his parents themselves needed to be convinced that his vocation was authentic. 'As I came to rationalize [my resistance] over the years,' he said, 'I can see that very much now, it's a sense of being, "I am a man of unclean lips", you know, I am unworthy, and I can't possibly do this.' It seemed, for a while, impossible to match the priestly models he had observed as a child, and he too struggled to measure himself against the ministers he believed that he knew best.

For women following a vocation to ordained ministry, difficulties are compounded by a lack of female role models, particularly at a senior level. Julie became increasingly conscious that she didn't fit herself into the widely accepted model of Anglican priesthood at all, identifying that as being male, professional and middle-class:

> I can't fit into any of those categories; I'm not male, I don't feel called to work in a middle-class setting, and I don't want to be professional in the sense of always getting it right.

Sarah, whose Evangelical understandings made it hard to accept a calling to priesthood, held on to the fact that 'God has called me to it, and so that is the bottom line.' Both women had no experiences of women's ordained ministry to draw upon, and no academic resources to help them deal with issues of gender and authority. Basing their expectations of what priesthood should be upon male figures (some of whom had expressed suspicion or doubt about the women's vocations) left them feeling vulnerable and confused. One woman, Andrea, admitted that she had entered ministry simply because she had seen a female priest coping well with the demands of parish and family: 'That's how I wanted to be', she said. It did not cross her mind that her journey to leading a parish might not be identical to that of the priest she so admired.

When ordinands talked about their initial stirrings of vocation, they often mentioned clergy whose example had inspired them to consider if they too might be called by God. There could be significant differences between the types of observed priesthood attractive to particular church traditions; a very crude generalization would be to say that Evangelical ordinands found inspiration in examples of 'successful' leadership while catholic ordinands responded to visions of 'holiness'; but whatever the underlying theology, it was the attractiveness of the example provided by particular priests that drove aspiring clergy to consider ordination. The individuals they had observed became templates of what dedicating oneself to Christian service could involve, and acted as 'ideal lives' in the sense that they suggested possibility and coherence. Surprisingly, it appears that these early images of ministry are not, as might have been expected, replaced during the discernment process with examples drawn from more recent experience, or from close and mature observation of other ordained people. The first figures to inspire admiration retain a powerful hold upon the imagination.[7] Yet if these 'ideal' images are not developed into more fully rounded models, ordinands are primed for discordance between what they believe and what they experience as they move through training and into parish life. They are left vulnerable to disappointment or even to the disintegration of their sense of calling.

Once vocations are accepted and affirmed by the Church, candidates for ordained ministry enter a period of compulsory ministerial training. It might be hoped that this will shape these idealized visions of priesthood into more realistic or sustainable forms. Students do not simply enter a new phase of education, but are preparing for a radically – and permanently – changed life; the experience of training for ordination is designed both to test their vocation and to form them into people who will adequately serve and represent the Church of England.[8] There may not be a single approved image of what a priest may be, but there are firm expectations that a particular way of life and being will be inculcated during training in order to equip ordinands for their future ministries. It seems, however, that taught theories of ministry cannot supplant embedded notions of 'proper' practice, and that although the experience of living and training with like-minded others is important ('truth emerges', claims Archdeacon Malcolm Grundy, 'in community'),[9] it is the expectations that ordinands already hold which affect both their reactions to the training process and the reference points against which they measure the 'success' of their progress. The models of priesthood which they have already internalized have the potential to affect the development of personal resources which they will carry forward into ministry.

Common responses to entering ministerial training can be summarized as follows:

1. God has called me here, God will be with me throughout this, and so all will be well.
2. The journey here has been complex and at times painful, and I am not yet sure that I am in the right place or doing the right thing.
3. I have responded reluctantly to a sense of vocation, I expect to be miserable much of the time, and I don't expect either training or ministry to be anything other than difficult.
4. I know that I am already competent and understand what ministry will be like, so I am just here to fulfil the unnecessarily bureaucratic demands of the Church.
5. I am pleased to be here, but I am uncertain about my ability to cope with the academic, practical or personal demands of training.

Each category brings with it both promise and threat. John Paul Lederach has theorized that vocation involves what he terms 'the mystery of risk';[10] of finding one's way home by stepping out into the unknown. Beginning training for ordained ministry is a moment of risk that encompasses the immense mystery of God and the likelihood of change. Whether or not it is a positive time depends not just on the personality and background of each ordinand, but also on the way experiences during training fit with the expectations they already have.

For some ordinands, difficulties in training can clash with their theological understandings. An unhappy period at one college caused some students with Evangelical backgrounds to interpret events either as a form of divinely sanctioned cleansing, or as a result of the failure of certain people to listen to God's wishes. If they believed that God was active in the world, and that God had a purpose and a plan for each of them and for their theological college, then they were forced to make sense of what had happened in terms of God's intention rather than as a result of human failings or weakness. A male student did his best to hold together his previous experience in the secular business world and his theological expectations: 'I can see why changes had to be made [at a functional level], and I can see why people would be resistant to change,' he explained, but 'when you move into something, very quickly you should be asking God, how long do you want me here?' Change was, in his view, a necessary and Godly response to particular events, but any problems caused by such change were a direct result of some members of the community not asking the right questions of God.

Paul, who had such high hopes of his college and his future ministry, suffered a prolonged period of illness, which left him finding God 'very silent'. Unable to pray, unable to read the Bible, suffering 'the most amount of [spiritual] pain I've ever been through', Paul began the first term of his final year's training recognizing that he was lonely, with no energy to work, study or exercise, and thoroughly miserable:

> I can't leave, because God's called me to it, but I don't want to be here because I'm in pain. It's like being on the cross, that's all I can describe it [as]; I want to get off, but that's the only place I have to be.

Paul's college staff told him to take time to recover, and some suggested that his illness was a form of spiritual testing and growth, a 'dark night of the soul' as described by the medieval mystic St John of the Cross.[11] Although this gave Paul a way of retaining faith throughout God's apparent absence, his lack of exposure to the spiritual classics (which might have been more familiar to someone with a catholic heritage) meant that he was left feeling angry that no one had warned him that periods of doubt and spiritual darkness were commonplace: 'It was like they expected it, they weren't surprised, which was quite frustrating. It's like they kept it secret.' His theology led him to believe that he was being 'disciplined' by God for a benevolent purpose: 'the Word tells you, no child likes to be disciplined by his father, and though they hate it, it's for their own good', and his sense of calling to a ministry of public evangelism was badly undermined. Instead of formation, he had suffered destruction, but his images of success-ful ministry had not changed. Instead, he believed sadly that he was not equal to the task set before him: 'God wrestles [hopes] off us.'

Part-time students on local training courses often intended to take up non-stipendiary ministries in their home parishes. For them, priesthood was intimately tied up with the places they knew best, and the clergy they observed there. Deborah, married to a parish priest, believed that she already knew what ordination would entail:

> [I understand] the sort of expectations of the parish on their clergy, the demands in terms of phone calls and knocks on the door at all times ... we've been public property for so long I've forgotten what it is not to be!

and saw her future as being 'a sort of Sunday helping out with ser-vices sort of role'. She did not expect that her life or her identity would be significantly changed by ordination, or that there would be any surprises along the way. Jonathan, who had led a church plant for some years, viewed ordination as conferring authority to full-time leadership rather than a calling in its own right. Priest-hood, he believed, was an administrative requirement that would allow the church plant to become a church in its own right; a demand of the Church rather than of God. He had no expecta-tions of being shaped or changed by the process. This is not true of *all* local students; Nicola chose part-time training so that she could continue to contribute to the family income, but was pre-paring for full-time stipendiary ministry. Also married to a serving priest, she insisted on gaining experience in unfamiliar parishes both during training and in her curacy. The shaping of her vision of priesthood was for Nicola both a hope and a necessity.

For students of a catholic understanding, the 'ideal' vision of priesthood was most commonly held alongside a theology that expects ordination to confer ontological change through the work of the Holy Spirit. Naomi had experienced a sudden and unexpected calling to the priesthood after the death of an ordained relative. She was accepted for training, but remained adamant that she was not called to parish ministry, having instead a 'contemplative and reflective' vocation. She clung to the hope that her future would, through the action of God, become clearer in time, but faced ordination with a sense of apprehension and a continuing uncertainty about what it meant to be called to be a priest. The images she held of priestly ministry did not fit with her understanding of her own abilities and gifts. Ordinands in the catholic tradition were, perhaps, less inclined than their Evangelical counterparts to be concerned about issues such as their motives in wishing to be ordained – in simplistic terms their theology suggested that surrender to the transforming influence of the Holy Spirit was more important than agonizing over whether they had been drawn to ordination because of worldly ambition – but were similarly keen to look forwards rather than consciously investigating the theoretical or experiential data that might refine their expectations. Simon, for example, talked of the 'inner compulsion' that had always made ordination seem unavoidable, even at its most unlikely, and of his belief that there is 'a difference between being a priest and doing ministerial things'. Lydia spoke of the need to spend time 'working out who I am' (with the implication that she was in the process of being changed by ordination training and by attention to God), and James analysed his understanding of priesthood as 'being made to be different for God'. They were concerned primarily with being shaped into something new by the activity of the Holy Spirit, and so saw as irrelevant the experiences of other people in particular places. The models of priesthood that had underpinned their initial vocations would remain as exemplars unless God acted to change their understandings.

There is a tendency for religious believers to try to fit their personal histories into the story of their faith tradition, and by this, claim membership of a group that is linked by the past (often expressed through ritual), the present and the (hoped for) future. Sociologist Danièle Hervieu-Léger describes this process as a 'chain of memory',[12] and believes that the accuracy of what is remembered or invoked is less important than the fact that it thereby allows individuals to feel part of the wider whole. She believes that the role of the priest is to *control* the way in which religious memories are utilized,[13] and so the way in which the ordained identify their place in the lineage of the faithful – in other words, how they insert their own stories into the doctrinally and socially constituted system in which they are authorized to teach and lead – has implications for their professional and personal understandings of priesthood. This could help to explain the power that those early models of 'ideal' priesthood hold in the imagination of those seeking ordination. Although the Church might expect that the long period of time investigating the 'realistic and informed'[14] nature of each vocation and training individuals for ordained ministry would act to shape and develop expectations of priestly identity, research suggests that this is not the case. The question 'Who shall I be?' remains focused on figures who acted as an inspiration in the earliest stages of exploring Christian vocation.[15] There is no guarantee that following their example will lead to contentment or capability.

There is one aspect of pre-ordination training that does seem to alter the idealistic nature of models of ordained ministry: that of practical, lived experience of different situations. Weekly and Sunday placements during theological training, substantial immersion in different church cultures before selection for ministry, or long placements during the summer vacations, all have the potential to have a significant impact on understandings and expectations. Sarah, whose faith had been shaped in a conservative Evangelical setting, found it impossible at first to reconcile her vocation and her long-held views about headship and obedience. It was only after moving to another diocese and being given responsibility for 'evangelism and nurture' in her new church, that she had the confidence to set aside the images of (male) ordained leadership with which she was familiar. During theological training, she spent a summer not in the Evangelical settings she knew best, but in a rural cluster of Anglo-catholic parishes. She knew that aspects of their theology might cause her some difficulty ('I spoke to my spiritual director before I went about ... things like the theology of the sacraments, praying for the dead and that sort of thing') and was daunted on her first Sunday to 'dress up in an alb', but found that the experience of talking through doctrinal understandings with the parish incumbent, and of experiencing a faith that was based around sacrament and routine practice, gave her an insight into a previously unformed aspect of her Christian faith. 'By the end of my six weeks there,' she said, 'having done the Daily Office and had Communion probably four or five times a week, I felt so spiritually sustained ... it's undergirded me.' Sarah realized that her theology and that of her Catholic host were 'not so far apart' and began to value the role of the Church in small communities so much that her hopes for future ministry were radically re-envisaged.

Full-time residential students are routinely offered such opportunities to experience new parish settings, different theological understandings, and some of the variety of work available to clergy. Martha, initially very unsure about where she should serve her title as a curate, was convinced that the placements she had been given during training had both confirmed her calling to priesthood and opened the possibility of working in rural areas: 'If I hadn't had the opportunity for placements and things like that, it wouldn't have happened in the same way ... [through placements] I've really grown, learned about weaknesses, strengths, where I keep seeing the influence of God.' Matthew affirmed that through a combination of 'academic studies, placements and personal development' his vocation had become 'clearer, it's taking shape'. Yet the part-time students on local courses who took part in this research project, often engaged in secular employment during the week and expecting to maintain contact with their sending parishes at weekends and during the holidays, did not routinely have this experience. It has already been noted that ordinands training locally tend to have very firm ideas about the future expression of their vocation; it seems unlikely that the theoretical examination of other situations, settings and understandings will have the same impact as residential ordinands report from placements elsewhere. They deserve more.

Alongside the development of individuals' understandings of what priesthood is or can be, and how it can be lived out, must run the beliefs and needs of the Church (both local and institutional) and the people whom they serve. Bruce Reed's work on the dynamics of Christian faith and its expression has demonstrated that religious institutions may be held together by shared understandings, but that these constitutive ideas are never static; they are continually 'reinforced, repaired and updated'.[16] For priesthood to be both authentic and sustainable, it must be based upon the belief that the fundamental understandings that underpin that priesthood *and also underpin the expressed faith of the Church which allows and authorizes it* are effective, powerful and culturally relevant.[17] This does not mean that Christianity or Christian priesthood are not based on deep and timeless concepts, but insists that the ideas which flesh out the way in which faith is practised and understood at a particular time and place will necessarily be affected by context and situation. If priests do not have confidence that they are representing something meaningful and effective, then, says Reed, they can become plagued by doubt, become dependent on others or defensive of their position and authority, or misuse their position to serve themselves rather than the Church. The skills and gifts of priestly individuals are crucial, but so is the responsiveness of the institutional Church to the needs of the world. Uncertain and underperforming priests can be the sign of an institution which is unsure of its role in a changing world.

Today's clergy have been described as exhibiting 'a profound (if implicit) sense of bewilderment'.[18] Aware that the models of the past are no longer achievable (if they ever were) and that many contemporary texts about priesthood reflect idealism rather than reality, they struggle to balance mythologized identities against their lived experience and attempt to maintain a sense of infinite possibility in the face of the limited reality of the present. We long to bring about change, but are too uncertain of who we are or where we stand to have the courage to act. For clergy, ambiguity about their identity and status can be both painful and disabling. Priesthood is more than ministry: it implies a state of being as well as the performance of particular tasks; yet the increasing professionalization of ordained ministry in a fast-changing and sceptical world leaves clergy bereft and bewildered. Questions about what it means to become a priest and how to shape a sustainable ministerial identity – 'Who shall I be and what shall I do?' – are crucial elements of the transition to ordained ministry. 'Putting on priesthood' must involve more than the assumption of an imagined (and sometimes imaginary) idealized identity. It can be nothing less than complete integration of the personal, the public and – above all – the possible.

Notes

1. *Country Life*, 22 September 2005, front cover.
2. *The Times Magazine,* 17 December 2005, front cover.
3. See Matthew Engelke and Matt Tomlinson, *The Limits of Meaning: Case Studies in the Anthropology of Christianity*, Oxford: Berghahn Books, 2007, p. 5, on religion as a 'cultural system' and the need for attention to issues of 'discipline, authority and power'.
4. See, for example, Michael Hinton's *The Anglican Parochial Clergy: A Celebration*, London: SCM Press, 1994, p. 12, which regrets the tendency towards 'individualism but less than formerly to eccentricity' in today's clergy.
5. Amanda Bloor, PhD thesis, 2012 (unpublished).
6. All names have been changed in order to preserve anonymity.
7. Billings notes that such images are difficult to 'overcome or modify significantly'. See Alan Billings, *Making God Possible: The Task of Ordained Ministry Present and Future*, London: SPCK, 2010, p. 167.
8. Priesthood, once conferred by ordination, cannot be revoked, although authority to exercise that priesthood on behalf of the Church can be withdrawn.
9. Malcolm Grundy, *What They Don't Teach You at Theological College*, Norwich: Canterbury Press, 2003, p. 13.
10. John Paul Lederach, *The Moral Imagination: The Art and Soul of Building Peace*, Oxford: Oxford University Press, 2005, p. 163.
11. James Bentley, *A Calendar of Saints*, London: Little, Brown and Company, 1997, p. 240: 'The saint describes how a mystic loses every earthly attachment, passing through a personal experience of Jesus' crucifixion to a rhapsodic union with God's glory. To pass through this darkness is, he says, "a fortunate adventure to union with the Beloved".'

12. Danièle Hervieu-Léger, *Religion as a Chain of Memory*, Norwich: Polity Press, 2003.

13. Hervieu-Léger, *Religion as a Chain of Memory*, p. 126. She draws a clear distinction between the 'mobilization of memory' by the priest and by a prophet. It should be noted that her studies are rooted in the context of predominantly Roman Catholic France, and that the boundaries in England may not be so clearly drawn.

14. *Summary of the Criteria for Selection for Ordained Ministry in The Church of England*, http://www.churchofengland.org/media/56413/Summary%20of%20Criteria.pdf-Micros (accessed 29 May 2012).

15. By which I mean the responsive discipleship asked of all Christians, not just a vocation to ordained ministry.

16. Bruce Reed, *The Dynamics of Religion: Process and Movement in Christian Churches*, London: Darton, Longman & Todd, 1978, pp. 42–43.

17. Reed describes these understandings as 'myths and symbols'. *The Dynamics of Religion*, p. 172.

18. Martyn Percy, *Clergy: The Origin of Species*, London: Continuum, 2006, p. 7.

3

Growing into Responsibility

IAN AVEYARD

This chapter is informed by a research project undertaken in 2010 and 2011 for the Church of England's Ministry Council. Besides a quantitative analysis through questionnaires we sought to interview, at some depth, 30 newish incumbents, a similar number of curates just finishing their training, and students just before they became curates. We covered a good cross-section of the Church of England. The material is grouped under three main headings, each relating to changes in understanding brought about during the last century. It also draws heavily on my experience of incumbency (25 years) in vastly different parishes, 20 years in theological education and 10 as Director of Ordinands (dual roles having the advantage of extending one's experience).

The breadth of Christian ministry

Among Church of England clergy there are several main models of ministry, each emanating from a major strand of church tradition and ecclesiology. (We speak positively of it as a 'broad church' implying a seamless spectrum, but it is more a coalition of four or more separate streams of tradition.) Nearly all are agreed that they have a duty of being the link between the worldwide Church and the local one, a ministry that is, in the words of the bishop at an institution 'both yours and mine'. Being the chaplain to the community, taking its marriages and funerals, is also accepted.

However, there are disparate views. Some see themselves as a Christian 'presence' in the community, endeavouring to be a human sign of the kingdom of God's values, and encouraging others to aspire to these high principles. They set great store by being at the day centre, with the scouts, and campaigning for the marginalized. Other clergy are primarily concerned with encouraging faith in believers and challenging those with none. They resolve to preach well, teach the faithful and encourage devotion. These two strands of ministry become almost mutually exclusive. Most clergy associate strongly with one or other of these two patterns, lacking a deep appreciation of the other and being unable or unwilling to add the other's insights to their ministry. The research strongly suggests that training, rather than widening, had the effect of narrowing these perspectives. Even those courses which deliberately sought to broaden student outlooks were less effective than they imagined.

The newest form of the ordinal has the words 'Guided by the Spirit, they are to discern and foster the gifts of all God's people, that the whole Church may be built up in unity and faith.' Few have yet to see themselves in this light: encouragers and empowerers of the church member's gifting, and co-ordinators of mission.

The environment in which we minister has changed dramatically over the last few generations. Population movement means that within our benefices or chaplaincies we are called to minister to Christians from different church backgrounds. The amalgamation of parishes into benefices means many clergy are working in groups of parishes with quite different theological outlooks and traditions. In these relatively new situations a more comprehensive practice and an inclusive theology are helpful, even perhaps necessary.

Where I was incumbent two decades ago the church community was expanding quickly, not primarily by transfers but with individuals coming to faith. In one short period I remember three people asking for help. One, from far outside the Church, gave me just a few minutes in which to explain what it was to be a Christian in the simplest possible language. A simple 'evangelical' presentation was appropriate. Another had been a Christian earlier in life and had gone 'into a far country'. This person was assisted back through formal confession and absolution. Another, again from outside the Church, had a most strange religious experience which needed affirmation, and then help in connecting it with orthodox Christian faith. Each of these incidents of ministry sprang from a different ecclesiology: evangelical, catholic and charismatic.

Widening the perspective

All these main models of ministry have a long and honoured tradition in the Church. 'Moving on', growing in ministry, necessitates an affirmation of the perspectives we already have, an acknowledgement of the narrowing that our training may have engendered, and a decision to value and embrace the perspectives that other traditions affirm, so that we can minister to as many as possible. This style of ministry can draw on more resources to address what is needed in a particular place at a specific time. I remember being deeply saddened listening to one assiduous priest, beloved by many, who assured me that in every parish he had served (and there were quite a few) his great achievement was to move its worship a few notches towards one end of the churchmanship spectrum.

Part of the problem is that academic training teaches us to discriminate between differing viewpoints, and establish which is more nearly correct. We become 'stuck' with the perspective we consider comfortable or more nearly correct. As a former theological educator, it seems to me we are better at enabling students to identify in what respects viewpoints are accurate than we are at teaching them how to integrate differing perspectives, and thus to embrace paradoxical truths.

In my university years I studied maths and physics, not the obvious academic background to equip a person for ministry. As well as being trained to think with clarity and precision, I was taught that the twentieth-century discoveries showed the world is not as it appears. Neils Bohr, the father of quantum mechanics, said, 'If quantum mechanics hasn't profoundly shocked you, you haven't understood it yet.' Of more significance to the minister is Bohr's statement, 'The opposite of a fact is falsehood, but the opposite of one profound truth may very well be another profound truth.'

God's creation is surprisingly paradoxical, where truths have to be held in tension. 'God is Trinity' does not invalidate 'God is One'. We have experience of handling 'many-eyed' truth for we have four authoritative Gospels, each giving a different perspective on Jesus of Nazareth. We need to bring 'many-eyed' truth into our everyday thinking. For example, how do we create a ministerial life that is equally informed by the synoptic 'kingdom of God' and the Johannine 'new birth'?

The controlling narrative

The research findings pose a serious question: What causes this apparent narrowing of understanding during training? The interviews I conducted indicated one main issue. The experience surrounding our 'call' too easily becomes a 'controlling narrative', with an associated limited ecclesiology. The call of God to ministry is unique for each of us. He knows what will seize our attention, and what vision will enable us wholeheartedly to surrender our present and embrace an unclear future. Perhaps we have the example of a priest we have admired, or the prospect of caring for people, or we are touched by a sermon. The research demonstrated that whatever way God seized our attention, and enabled us to pursue his invitation, we value the vision immensely. The drawback is that we fail to recognize the initial invitation as a summons to a much wider prospect: that of taking our part in the fullness of ministry in God's Church. Our ministry may have specialisms for which we are particularly gifted. However, its representative nature requires us both to expand our understanding and also to nurture our giftedness in order, however imperfectly, to reflect the breadth of God's mission to his world. With the immensity of the task and the urgency of many tasks, rather than grasping the bigger picture we tend to revert to the initial vision. For example, if we were called through the life of a particular minister, his or her ideals may have become our vision, instead of us reflecting God's mission in that particular place.

We noted many other hindering factors, of which I mention two more. There are often implicit pressures from those who supported or sponsored us for ministry. If we have trained without moving home, we are likely to be subject to significant pressures from some of those remaining in the church and community. Change in us is felt as criticism of them. The divine call to 'move on' can encourage us to bear their negative evaluation of us, with the knowledge that broad shoulders, if not a thick skin, will be needed in the future. In residential theological training the peer group pressures are great. We desire to be accepted among those we value. Moreover, in a time of great transition, when the need to belong is huge, close friendships are formed. Few of us have the courage to risk these new relationships by exploring what others are insistent is misguided, erroneous or even heretical.

As we move into ministry we find there is much to do, with seemingly unlimited calls upon our time and energy. With little to spare with which to attend to the truths of others, we are tempted to avoid the paradoxes they involve. Instead, it seems, we miss the deeper questions that our situation evokes and gravitate to the simplistic. Under pressure we fall too easily into patterns of thought and practice that are, in effect, one-dimensional answers to complex communal, pastoral or personal problems. Since conducting the research, the Church of England has agreed a new process of formative assessment through curacy. Whether this new procedure encourages a dynamic engagement with those of other traditions or simply gaining enough experience to 'tick the box' will only be discovered in time.

How might we help ourselves? We have high ideals so want to grow in our ministries. This requires two disciplines. First, it needs consistent and profound reflection upon our experience, both positive and negative. In the technical language of education, we need to attend to the cognitive dissonance. Second, embracing the dissonance will require changes in ministerial practice. We may need to be willing to leave behind established habits to discover what is good and bad about new possibilities, whether that is in how we visit, take a funeral or chair the church council. We may also need to give ourselves 'permission', through a widened theology, before trying out these different ways.

The leadership of incumbency

The research we undertook was precipitated by the observation of some senior clergy that the training process was not producing the incumbents whom bishops wished to appoint to a parish or bene-fice. The project was designed to identify the factors involved. One facet which was particularly noticeable was the discrepancy between the firm confidence of the curates at the end of their train-ing and the deep concerns of the cohort of incumbents. The 'mood music' of these cohorts, two or three years apart, was entirely dif-ferent. The short years of being 'in charge' had evoked multiple issues and questions for which they felt inadequately trained.

'Moving on' usually means, at some stage, taking responsibility for a parish, benefice or chaplaincy. Instantly, the role becomes much more complex with an interplay of many factors, few previ-ously faced: decision making, leadership, the difference between theory and practice, meeting resistance to change, balancing the segments of the post, expectations of ourselves and others, hold-ing, delegating and relinquishing power, the ability to prioritize, the needs of family and friends, loneliness, external support, and measuring achievement.

One need is for high-quality discernment. How do ministers and people determine what is needed when churches want no less than the Archangel Gabriel, have a range of wholly unreasonable expectations, and a minister who wants, if not to shine, to be considered better than satisfactory? We are faced with decisions about the proportions of time spent on the various aspects of our role: presence in the community, building up the church, pastoral care, and mission. Honest and realistic conversations, creating a collaborative strategy, are needed, but all too rare. Moving on fruitfully in ministry requires integrity, determination and clear thinking to 'make his paths straight'. If relentless activity is avoided to allow for deeper thoughtfulness, we may be consid-ered less than wholly enthusiastic. Getting the right balance is not easy between practical jobs: discussing the church fabric report with the architect, sending publicity to the printers and organizing the preaching rota, and what might seem the more 'ministerial' roles: visiting the housebound, sermon preparation, and praying.

However, avoiding the issue leads to a mis-match between vision and decision making, misunderstandings between the various partners: parish, community, minister and diocese, and a lack of internal spiritual and psychological coherence in the clergyperson. This latter leads to a lack of effectiveness and can occasionally result in burnout.

The question of whether leadership is automatically associated with ordained ministry has clouded discussion over the years. Some have maintained that the fundamental functions of preaching or celebrating the Eucharist do not require leadership skills. Without prejudice to that discussion, the research concludes that taking charge of a benefice or chaplaincy requires considerable leadership. We can effectively minister for Christ as a priest but once we 'take charge', leadership is required. Having experienced this need, three-quarters of the newish incumbents we surveyed wanted to enhance these skills. Leadership requires a kaleidoscope of essential competences such as astute observation, creating corporate vision, generating strategy from vision, collaborative implementation of policy, prioritization, communication and team building. All these individual skills are necessary, and growth into 'taking charge' requires their continual enhancement.

Expanding the territory

The step-up to being an incumbent (or anywhere else the buck stops) is always considerably larger than expected. We might anticipate quantitative differences, more hours and bigger decisions, but the surprise is that it is qualitatively different. There is a series of stakeholders with whom we now need to work. In the case of a parish: local councillors, the clergy of other churches both in the benefice and in the wider area, leaders of the British Legion, local social workers, diocesan boards and advisers. The new chaplain will have to forge similar relationships with the institution's leadership, staff, clients' representatives, local office-holders and others. Our ministry will be tested not only by the decisions we make but also by the quality of relationships we create. This is not just the experience of clergy. Those who take charge, from the company CEO to the head teacher, find that functioning where the buck stops, with its much wider perspectives, responsibilities and connections, takes on a different quality from assistant posts, however all-consuming.

When reflecting on their training we heard that there was insufficient focus on the practicalities of ministry. It was noted that the majority of the teaching was provided by very able academics who had, unfortunately, insufficient practical experience of ministry, especially that of being 'in charge'. The real challenge is to make good connections between theology and the practical life of the church. For example, how does the minister who believes in the appropriateness of infant baptism bridge the gap between his or her theological beliefs and the parents who want baptism for their child only to enable the wider family to say 'Welcome'. The writings of Donald Schön on professional life show that the relationship of academic understanding to practical professional life is often not well made.[1] In most disciplines there is a significant gap between what he called 'high hard ground' of academic knowledge and 'swampy lowlands' of the real human concerns and questions. At its best, ministerial life can encourage integrity between the high ground and lowlands, but too often clergy hold one at the expense of the other.

Many times during the interviews I heard clergy say, 'I was not ordained for this.' The issue is that there may be a considerable gap between the high language of the ordinal and some routine aspects of the minister's life. The newish incumbents told us that being 'in charge' brings more administration, greater time in representing the Church, and significant internal mediation. To many, these unavoidable tasks of the incumbent were not primarily what they had in mind when they offered for ministry. Yet they are vital, if only for underpinning the 'real' work. Whatever we anticipated, throughout the training process these routine tasks were part of the ordaining church's expectation. We can take some comfort from the fact that this discrepancy is present in other professions, for example, the teachers who wish to continue at the chalk-face and not take on further responsibilities. If we allow our initial vision of ministry to continue to be determinative then this frustration can do nothing but grow. On the other hand, we might conclude that God knew that these chores would be included in our tasks, and our call to ordination included them. Additionally, there is a constant temptation to place our own gifting centre-stage. We are the Church's representatives, not independent clergy doing our own thing (no matter how good we are). Other professions know this too, for example the university professor who is more concerned for his or her own research rather than the prestige of the university.

Most of us go through our training with little change to our understanding of ministry and mission. Consequently, we should not be surprised at how resistant others are to change, even in the smallest things. Real change in a community, where its culture shifts significantly, requires long and patient work. Late on in my days as an incumbent I overheard a conversation between two 80-year-olds reminiscing about the clergy they had known in 'their' parish. As they recollected the past 75 years, they were very astute about the idiosyncrasies of each incumbent, and it proved entertaining. However, the subtext of the whole conversation was, 'We were tolerant with them, and eventually they left, and we carried on just as before.' If we considered such resistance as normal then we might be less hasty to create cosmetic change, instead patiently planning for a few profound transformations.

Responding to the challenge

At this 'step-up' we soon recognize the people who want the lion's share of our attention. We must indicate that we have listened well and taken careful note, while having the wisdom and resolution to know when to communicate a disappointing 'No'. Encouraging evolutionary change calls for patience, but also resolute determination in the face of other forces; from those on one extreme wanting revolution to the other end of the spectrum where change is believed unnecessary. The minister's task is to hold the whole community together, being a focus for unity, while seeking to move it on. There will be those who let us know, at times quite candidly, they are in disagreement with us and yet they are the ones in whom we most need to encourage confidence in our leadership. We will spend disproportionate amounts of time and energy keeping them on board. Setting the 'mood music' for evolutionary change is an ongoing feature of many conversations, preaching, teaching and decision making. Since we deal with fallible people, and most of all we know our failings, it will never be perfect, but we learn through many 'near misses' to have a sense of what will be sufficiently right. Just occasionally there will be the need for something more revolutionary, which will call for a different set of skills and courage.

The changes in the environment of ministry, particularly the pressures to merge posts, are here to stay. Holding together disparate roles and different expectations is a huge challenge, for which there can be little preparation. There is a huge temptation to favour the part of the post fitting more nearly our own predispositions. Resistance to this temptation and a determination to embrace the other parts of the role may be of enormous long-term benefit. In my last stipendiary role I held a three-quarter time diocesan post with the incumbency of a parish which included a challenging council housing estate. One of the hardest, yet most satisfying, features was the switching, intellectual and emotional, between *The Times* and the *Sun* several times a day.

In the second half of the twentieth century there seemed to be a growing theological consensus, in both ARCIC and Lima conversations, that the fundamental locus for 'priestliness' is not the minister but the local community of faith. In *The Gospel in a Pluralist Society* Lesslie Newbigin described the congregation as 'the hermeneutic of the gospel'.[2] If this consensus, from such differing perspectives, is accurate, we need to turn our focus away from ourselves to the community of faith. Whether one is concerned with defining 'success' or 'achievement' or planning the day-to-day priorities, it is what the faith community is becoming that is primary. This is cognitively and psychologically hard because most of our pilgrimage into ministry has placed our call centre-stage.

Whether our personal theology allows for it or not, the minister is often perceived to be the embodiment of God. Whatever view one takes on the 'icon of Christ', a version of the idea is firmly held by many members of the community (and sometimes, seemingly, in proportion to their distance from church affiliation). A good example is the way in which many bereaved people will express their anger towards the minister who has come to arrange the funeral: it being more than disconcerting to have one's compassion met with hostility. This projection complicates many relationships, as clergy perfection is expected, yet unavailable. The newly trained learn this during their first years in ministry. However, when 'in charge' the pressure increases dramatically, as we are now (somehow) held personally responsible for the activities, not only of God, but also all members of the church community.

Taking charge of the 'power'

Leadership also requires a delicate balance between holding, delegating and relinquishing power. We have various power sources: the institution of the Church, any organization we may work for, our knowledge and competence, and our own personal stature. The *Common Worship* ordinal has the words 'Guided by the Spirit, they are to discern and foster the gifts of all God's people, that the whole Church may be built up in unity and faith.' For the growth of 'all God's people' power and responsibility will need to be delegated to them. How much will be a matter of judgement. Too little and the minister becomes the limiting factor for growth. Too much and there may be little direction and co-ordination. Inevitably, it is complicated because those to whom it is delegated will believe they know much better than the vicar how to minister well. Judgement in this is not something we can learn from the textbooks, for much of it is a function of who we are ourselves, our sense of the divine 'delegation' to us, and our perception of the community in which we are set. A parish of 'Chiefs' and no 'Indians' may be as problematical as one where there are no 'Chiefs'. Those disgruntled may well contact senior clergy with their complaints, so wisdom also dictates we weigh the bishop's probable reaction. 'Moving on' in this aspect of leadership is a lifetime's journey.

Our strategy includes discovering where power is held. From the office we hold we have institutional power, but in any community there are those who hold associational power. We have only to observe a group decision being made, when its members monitor one person's views before making a decision, to know where that power is held. In a small church community, inadvertently challenging that associational power is a serious blunder. When it needs to be done openly, we must be aware of the likely consequences.

In any leadership there is a measure of loneliness. Some things one cannot discuss with anyone remotely involved. One aspect of our growth is to have someone external to whom everything can be told, warts and all, who will be a wise confidant, critical friend, mentor, encourager, and who will give clear feedback. This is more than the traditional role of the spiritual accompanier. The identification of such a person may not be easy, but it is vital. Unfortunately, the curacy experience may not have created a good model as there can be a generational discrepancy between the curate and incumbent, not in age but in worldview.

Changes in society also propel us towards external support. The erosion of the numbers belonging to the church, and the discounting of religious experience within the wider community, can cause clergy to feel that their contribution to society is much less than the personal cost involved. This culture, sitting lightly to its Christian heritage, leaves clergy needing greater support. I have valued belonging to a clergy cell group meeting monthly both for encouragement and (occasional) challenge.

Encouragement often comes through feeling valued. How will we judge ourselves at the end of the day, week, month or year? What are the criteria? Can the criteria be objective enough for an impartial assessment? Whether we make an accurate self-assessment or not, others will measure us numerically. Most of us are aware that we are expected to generate numerical success: numbers visited, appointments made, weddings taken, communicants at Christmas. We are also aware that most of the growth factors leading to numerical 'success' are not ours to control. If numbers are suspect, so too is an assessment based on the apparent contentment of a congregation. They may be getting what they want, or alternatively may be resigned to never getting it, or getting what they want even if something else is really required. 'Moving on' requires an honest, hubris-free, assessment of 'success' and 'failure', with realistic plans for continual improvement.

Theology and psychology in tandem

The research project identified more than educational and structural issues; some were more psychological. Ministry is hugely demanding. The cost is not just tiredness, but often frustration at so little achievement. From time to time, we will be wounded by the encounters. Unless we take proper account of the injury, the natural reaction will be to protect ourselves better, and to guard against similar encounters. We may need help, and time, for this process. If not, over the years the walls around us will be built, and those to whom we minister will meet a shadow of the real person. Just occasionally the wounding is so great that we may need to seek a different form of ministry, temporarily or even permanently. Those who have the task of taking many funerals are especially vulnerable to the hardening that arises from a failure to process the grief involved. We may think that an appropriate professional 'distance' will protect us. However, a sufficient 'distance' to prevent impact is too great for empathetic listening. In addition, belonging to a community, the loss of that community's members is bound to bring personal grief. Consistently we must remember that the treasure is in earthen vessels.

In the last century psychology has confirmed what the Gospels indicated: that what matters is the quality of the meeting of one person with another. It is neither the right words nor even the right deeds that minister; it is through who we are, and have become, that God touches others. Learning this lesson of the personal encounter can take years, particularly as we move it from our heads to our hearts. As a student I was impressed by a friend whose hospital bedside manner seemed effective, with just the right words. Eventually I learnt that my reticence could also be good for patients, sometimes giving opportunity for a deeper encounter.

With constant demanding encounters, retaining a good and growing emotional life is one of the great challenges of long-term ministry. With the work/life balance under pressure most of us need more 'time out' than we feel legitimate to take. Added to which, as there are fewer ministers and spheres of ministry grow, the balance of our work tilts towards the more demanding; the less essential, and often easier, being jettisoned. In some occupations usefulness may not be compromised if one's emotional life shrivels, but in Christian ministry effectiveness is diminished too. 'Moving on' requires great care over ourselves.

The growth of the psychological sciences leads also to revising some of our pastoral perspectives. We have a growing understanding of the connection between sin and being sinned against. We will find ourselves ministering to those who have been abused, and who come to us for help in their pilgrimage. Traditional pastoral practice has made little allowance for 'being sinned against', which in consequence means people may be further abused by our conduct – for example, inviting people too quickly to forgive those who show no awareness of their abusive behaviour, or using liturgies which imply that such forgiveness is a necessary precursor to God's mercy. Our traditional language is of sinners justified, but equally it needs to be of victims freed.

Communicating in a media age

The research provided some surprises. An interview question sought to discover how far clergy felt able to help congregations articulate their faith. In the majority of cases this elicited a 'confession'. Clergy told us they themselves were inhibited in articulating their beliefs outside the faith community. In our theological studies we do not seem yet to have considered carefully enough the implications of what one media academic has described as a new public discourse – 'one which privileges experience over knowledge, emotion over reason and popular opinion over expert advice'. Few of us who were taught to 'think theologically' have a language that embraces a 'theology of emotion and experience'. Perhaps we need to believe the evidence of our own training, where the greatest impact is usually the experience of the pastoral placement. There is a significant distance to travel, from the knowledge that mission is essential, to the reality of an authentic proclamation of the gospel in this different landscape.

'Moving on' in ministry is never a quick business. As I have outlined, it may require paradigm shifts in the breadth of what we offer, in the leadership we embrace and understanding the needs of the individuals involved. It is quite a challenge, but one worth accepting.

Notes

1. See, for example, Donald A. Schön, *The Reflective Practitioner: How Professionals Think in Action*, 1983; Aldershot: Ashgate, 1991.

2. Lesslie Newbigin, *The Gospel in a Pluralist Society*, London: SPCK, 1989.

4

Understanding and Enabling Clergy Careers

JANE STURGES

The working lives of Church of England clergy are subject to what are regarded as two potentially conflicting interests: calling and career. Priests are called by God to become ministers; from this perspective, they work for a purpose other than their own, dedicate themselves to work beyond self-interest and may believe that they have little choice over the form that their working life takes.[1] On the other hand, clergy working lives have many similarities with the careers of other professionals. They consist of a series of roles in which priests are engaged; they may involve increased responsibility and hierarchical progression; and the form they take can reflect individual preferences and choice. While previous writers have argued that the tension between the ideals of a calling and the secular demands of a career is potentially problematic,[2] this chapter proposes that reference to career theory can deepen understanding of clergy working lives and may help the successful deployment of clergy. It presents the findings of a Church of England-funded research study that used the framework of the career to explore clergy working lives, in order to gain insight into how they would like their ministry to develop and what factors might aid or hinder its development. The research was conducted within the work psychology discipline; this context means that the author provides an 'outsider' perspective on the working lives of clergy, which is intended to help give fresh insights regarding transitions into and through ministry.

Careers and callings

A career can be defined as the 'sequence of employment-related experiences encountered by a person'.[3] From the perspective of this broad definition, it is possible to conceptualize any working life as a career and to use the framework of the career to gain useful insights into work attitudes and behaviour. A central notion of career theory is that a career has meaning to both the individual pursuing an occupation and to their employer, in whose interests it is to develop individuals so that they can contribute to the organization.[4] Both aspects of the career are important for deepening understanding of clergy careers. Within the context of their calling, priests have career-related aspirations that may be poorly understood and neglected. Dioceses, on the other hand, need to make plans to develop and deploy the human resources that their clergy provide.

Individual career aspirations are often described in terms of career orientations. Career orientations theory[5] provides insight into what individuals working in managerial and professional roles want to achieve from their careers. Because career orientations reflect what individuals want from their careers they affect the career choices that people make – where they work, what type of jobs they want to do, and how their working lives develop.

The best-known theory of career orientations is Schein's Career Anchor theory,[6] which categorizes individuals according to the different types of career that they favour. Schein argues that people develop a career anchor – the basis from which their working life develops – according to their talents and abilities, motives and needs, and attitudes and values. Five career anchors were originally identified by Schein's research: *a technical and functional competence* anchor, where the individual's career is guided by a desire to emphasize the functional specialism of a job, for example, accountancy or law; *a managerial competence* anchor, where the individual's career is motivated by a desire to rise to positions of managerial responsibility; *a security and stability career* anchor, where the individual's career focuses on securing long-term stability; *a creativity career* anchor, where the individual's career develops from a desire for self-expression at work, for example, through the creation of a new business which can be closely identified with their own efforts; and *an autonomy career* anchor, where the individual's career is driven by a wish to be as free from organizational constraints as possible.[7] Later research led Schein to add a further three career anchors to his list: *a sense of service, dedication to a cause* anchor, where the individual's career is shaped more by strong moral values than actual talents and competencies; *a pure challenge* anchor, where the individual's career is dominated by a desire to seek high levels of challenge in their work; and *a lifestyle* anchor, where the individual's career is seen as an integral part of their total lifestyle.[8]

Research has also explored the career orientations of managers in terms of how they define career success on their own terms.[9] Four types of people have been identified: *the Climber* defines career success in objective terms, such as hierarchical position, promotion and reward, and often aspires to reaching the most senior levels of an organization; *the Expert* sees career success as achieving a high level of competency at their job and being recognized for being good at what they do, by being seen as an expert or by winning the respect of the people they work with; *the Influencer* defines career success as making an impact on their organization, but is not interested in status or reward for their own sake; *the Self-Realizer* does not measure their career success in any kind of organizational terms at all but defines it more in terms of personal fulfilment and achievement.

The career aspirations and orientations of Church of England clergy might be expected to differ from those of people working in other jobs, because their working life is predicated upon a vocation or calling.[10] Previous research has identified some characteristics of a calling as being psychological, as opposed to material, success,[11] service to the common good and experience of meaningfulness of work.[12] Such characteristics might be expected to lead to distinctive notions of career success.

The research study

The aim of the research on which this chapter is based was to address the following questions:

1. What does career success mean to Church of England clergy?
2. What factors prevent Church of England clergy from achieving the career success that they seek?
3. What factors enable Church of England clergy to achieve the career success to which they aspire?

The research was conducted as a qualitative study in three dioceses. Face-to-face, in-depth interviews were conducted with 36 stipendiary clergy from the three dioceses in the first quarter of 2011. In order to capture the views of male and female clergy at different ages and different career stages, the sample was drawn from three cohorts that represented different points in clergy careers. Interviews were conducted with five men and eight women in their post of responsibility, six men and six women in mid-ministry (ten years into their career), and seven men and four women in their last post.

What does career success mean to Church of England clergy?

The research showed that career success means different things to different people. Being a good priest, making a difference to people's lives and enabling them to achieve their own success were at the centre of many people's definition of career success. Nevertheless, for others, especially those later in their career, other success factors, such as influencing, leading and developing, were also important. Most participants did not view success in terms of hierarchical advancement, but they sometimes aspired to it for what it would offer them in terms of opportunities to influence, lead and develop. Two other factors emerged as significant influences on whether people felt successful or not. First, feedback and recognition were crucial, both from parishioners and from senior clergy. The latter was especially important for clergy later in their career. Second, some clergy believed that they would only feel successful if they were able to achieve a work–life balance as well as career success. The research identified a total of nine different conceptualizations of career success used by the clergy who took part in the study to define career success for themselves on their own terms. The nine conceptualizations are summarized in Figure 1 (p. 51).

Being a good priest

For some participants, especially a group of priests in their first post, career success was conceptualized primarily in terms of being a good priest. Defining success in this way related to doing the best job they could, in terms of leading services and pastoral work, but also involved spirituality and faithfulness. As one participant noted, 'a priest is something you are, not something you do', so that success in these terms, to quote another participant, felt 'spiritual, personal, emotional'. Experiencing success in terms of being a good priest was often linked to feelings of personal and vocational fulfilment, again especially for those early in their career.

> 'I just get a tremendous buzz and sense of fulfilment from the parish mass, there's nothing greater than being part of the body of Christ here, worshipping God with passion and joy and doing it well … when I say doing it well, I don't just mean doing it professionally with high standards but I mean, doing it in beauty and truth.'
>
> (Male, first post)

Making a difference

The most important marker of career success for some priests was feeling that they had made a difference to people's lives. This group included clergy at all stages of their career but comprised twice as many women as men. Sometimes making a difference

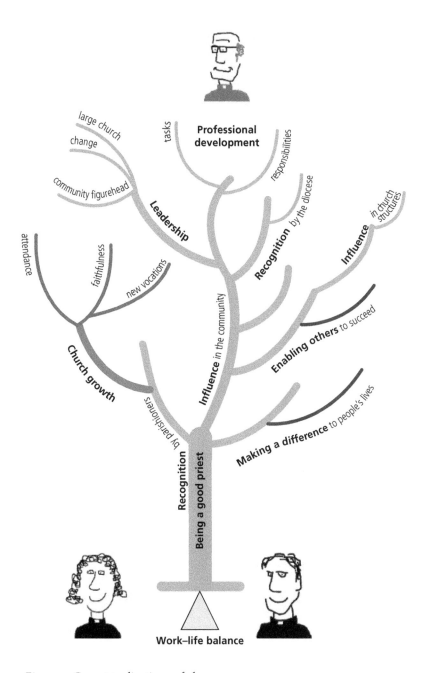

Figure 1. Conceptualizations of clergy career success

involved supporting people at difficult times of their lives, such as during an illness or bereavement. Priests commonly described this in terms of 'being alongside people' at such times. Other clergy felt that they were able to make a difference in people's lives by helping particular groups in the community, such as young people, or even by helping whole communities, for example through charity projects overseas.

> 'I think of success much more in terms of having made a difference to people's lives and seeing the spirit working their lives in small ways.'
>
> (Female, mid-career)

Enabling others

For many of the clergy interviewed, especially women, success in their career meant enabling other people to succeed, rather than achieving things for themselves. This kind of vicarious success was reflected in parishioners successfully undertaking tasks such as leading worship, visiting the sick and elderly and running voluntary groups, both in the church and in the wider community. Enabling this through facilitation, encouragement and support made priests in this group feel successful:

> 'I think I measure success as how much individuals within the church are taking on responsibility and handling it well and how much I am encouraging others to take up their ministry, whether it's making coffee or doing intercessions or whatever.'
>
> (Female, first post)

Church growth

An important criterion of career success for many clergy was church growth. Some, especially men, measured this chiefly in terms of the number of people who came to church services:

'It's very difficult not to count bums on pews – it is part of the picture. I'm not one of the people that say numbers don't matter at all.'

(Male, first post)

However, most people who saw success in terms of church growth were reluctant to focus on the number of people who came to church as a measure of success on its own, but deemed enabling growth in faith to be far more important.

'The numbers don't tell the whole story. Helping individuals grow in faith is what we do and that for me has always been the absolute priority.'

(Female, mid-career)

A third growth criterion used by some people to measure their success was the number of people from their parish putting themselves forward for ordination:

'I think we're now on to our fifth person who's thinking of going forward for ordination ... the church is clearly presenting something that's positive enough for other people to feel that they want to do the job, and that's encouraging.'

(Female, last post)

Influence

For some priests, career success meant being able to have an influence on the policy and behaviour of the Church of England at a diocesan or even a national level. This generally implied holding a senior position in the church hierarchy that would allow them to exercise this kind of influence. Some of this group were overt about their wish to become a bishop or an archdeacon, although most were adamant that they aspired to such positions because of the influence they would gain rather than for the status of a senior role. It is interesting to note that many people in this group had already had successful careers in other occupations before they were ordained.

'Success is being involved in the bigger decisions, being involved in strategy ... influence.'

(Female, first post)

Other people saw success in terms of a different kind of influence, being able to have a positive impact on the wider community where their church was located. This involved working with local schools and community groups to support the development of the local area. Many clergy who saw success in this way were in their first post.

'We want to transform the community, that's massively ambitious but it's also really inspiring. I love that sense of being part of that movement of transformation within a community.'

(Male, first post)

Leadership

Leadership was an important aspect of career success for some priests in their mid-career or last post. This was not linked to hierarchical advancement, although some clergy experienced career success through leadership by running a large church. Others saw it differently, in terms of being a community figurehead or successfully leading change.

'I would be lying if I didn't say it's satisfying to lead in a community and I think that is a real privilege and there is a real satisfaction that goes with that.'

(Female, mid-career)

Professional development

For many people in their mid-career or last post, career success was linked to feeling that they were continuing to develop as priests. There were different ways in which professional development was construed. For some, taking on additional responsibilities within their diocese was important. Other people liked to be able to undertake new projects that they found interesting and developmental. This was often linked to the belief that feeling successful resulted from undertaking challenging roles and tasks.

> 'I've taken on being a vocations adviser and I'm about to join the diocesan board of education. So in that sense I think there is a personal and profession growth.'
>
> (Male, mid-career)

Work–life balance

A group of clergy, most in their first post, believed that being able to balance their working life as a priest with their non-work life, especially with their family life, was an important aspect of career success for them. This was linked to the nature of priestly work, which people believed could consume their whole life in a way that might easily exclude other aspects of it. It also related to workload, which people felt had to be managed carefully if they were not to spend all their time working. Clergy in this group did not believe that they would be able to consider their careers as priests to be successful, if any achievement was at the expense of their well-being and their relationship with their family.

> 'The criterion for success is that I find that balance ... that I actually find the time and the energy and the resources for my own family ... but also find the time, the energy and the resources for the stuff that comes with ministry.'
>
> (Male, first post)

Recognition

For most of the participants, career success was not just about achievement, for example in terms of being a good priest or grow-ing the church. It was also important that this achievement was recognized through positive feedback and affirmation. Clergy at all stages of their career valued recognition of their work by their parishioners (although it was acknowledged that it was not always forthcoming).

'At last year's Annual General Meeting it was quite moving because one of the people who comes to the church just stood up and said she wanted to thank me for how I had become part of the community and for the work that I was doing. It's important for everyone to be affirmed in who they are, or what they are doing.'

(Female, first post)

Some people, especially those later in their career, believed that recognition by senior clergy in the diocese was particularly important, in terms of making them feel valued and successful. For some people, this took the form of being made a canon; for others it involved being given extra responsibilities or being selected to represent the diocese or the Church of England in a particular group or context.

'I was asked to go abroad as part of an ecumenical delegation and I remember feeling ... oh this is very good ... I must be quite important, and that's quite nice. So, that would be like a little measure of career success.'

(Female, last post)

What factors prevent Church of England clergy from achieving the career success that they seek?

Clergy identified four groups of factors as barriers that they believed prevented them from achieving the career success to which they aspired: personal attributes; diocesan support; people-management policy and practice; and workload.

Some of the women interviewed believed that being female had hindered their career development. While it was acknowledged that this may be less of an issue than it had been in the past, some women felt that they were not taken as seriously as their male colleagues and others believed that covert sexism still existed in the appointments system. Race was similarly identified as a factor that may be a barrier to individuals' career progression within the Church, for example by this male priest in his first post: 'I just think of people growing up in this congregation and I hope the church will one day reflect the people who are here on a Sunday morning in its leadership and its hierarchy because it just doesn't begin to at the moment.'

While some clergy were positive about the help that they received from archdeacons and bishops, others were more critical about the lack of support they had from within their diocese. This in part related to criticisms of review systems (discussed below), but also concerned diocesan structures, which meant that clergy did not have a 'line manager' to direct and support them. This was particularly identified as a problem by those early in their career, like this female priest. 'We don't really have a natural line manager that supervises you. So you have to be incredibly self-starting. I think as a bishop it would be good to look at some strategy and some systematic pastoral care, a more robust system of appraisal and supervision.' It was acknowledged that this was a specific consequence of diocesan structures, which meant that bishops had pastoral responsibility for large numbers of clergy.

A few participants believed that the Church did not have the people-management policies and practices necessary to ensure that clergy careers could flourish. From their perspective, diocesan systems were inadequate for the strategic planning and use of clergy. Participants identified specific aspects of this that they felt could be improved. First, some participants felt that the current appointments system did not work well in terms of finding the right person for the job, as this male priest in mid-career explains: 'I think there needs to be a much more open system of recruitment where vacancies are advertised and properly described. Getting a group of people in a parish to write an advert is never really going to tell you what it's like ... if you were the angel Gabriel and you worked overtime, then you might be the sort of person a lot of these parishes were looking for.' Many priests also believed that 'who you know' still mattered more than 'what you know' when it came to filling posts. Second, many participants expressed dissatisfaction with diocesan review systems, which they felt often lack continuity and left clergy feeling that their development was not taken seriously.[13] Third, some clergy felt that there needed to be more clarity about potential clergy career paths. One male priest in his last post noted: 'In terms of a career, there isn't one ... only what you make of it ... there is no career path.' It was suggested that, due to the difficulty of hierarchical progression, more attempts should be made to develop clergy careers in other ways, for example by giving people additional diocesan responsibilities. Finally, participants noted that they did not receive any help with managing their career. This meant that they needed to be proactive about their own career development, for example by getting on influential committees or by drawing senior clergy's attention to them and their achievements in other ways. A few interviewees believed that their career development had been hampered because they lacked the self-confidence to promote themselves in this way. Others disliked having to behave like this and were not prepared to do so, even if it was to the detriment of their career development.

Some clergy, particularly those who saw success primarily in terms of being a good priest and making a difference in people's lives, felt that a heavy workload (especially when they had to look after multiple parishes) made it difficult for them to achieve success on their terms:

> '... lack of time, lack of resources ... I think it's that sense of a never-ending job, so you can sometimes feel you haven't done the things you want to do. The multitude of tasks can sometimes be oppressive.'
>
> (Male priest, mid-career)

What factors enable Church of England clergy to achieve the career success to which they aspire?

The research found that clergy believed that two groups of factors were important in helping them to achieve the career success to which they aspired: help and support from people; and training and other developmental experiences. The research participants identified help and support from people as the most important influence on their career development as priests. Three specific kinds of support were noted: career support, personal support, and spiritual support.

Career support related to the kind of help that clergy needed to develop their careers, for example, help with on-the-job learning, career and vocational advice, and help with finding jobs. Important sources of support at the beginning of the career were seen to be the parish priest who encouraged and supported an individual's vocation, the Diocesan Director of Ordinands and theological college staff. The relationship that a priest had with their training incumbent in their curacy was seen to be particularly critical for career development, as described here by a male priest in his first post:

> 'He was brilliant at being a critical friend ... he got the balance just right of being with me doing things when I needed it, but also letting me go and doing things on my own when it was right, and I really appreciated that.'

Some people identified archdeacons and bishops in their diocese as a crucial source of career support for their development; for others, however, this kind of support was seen to be unforthcoming or difficult to access, as discussed above. Other kinds of career support identified were mentoring (although very few clergy had this kind of support) and help from a work consultant. All of the clergy interviewed pointed to personal support as one of the factors that had helped them most. Participants identified a number of sources from which they drew such support, for example family, friends and in particular clergy colleagues, who understood the kind of issues that they had to deal with in their work. Such a relationship is described here by a female priest in mid-career:

> 'I have a colleague who's been in ministry a lot longer than I have and she's real salt of the earth ... feet on the ground sort of person, a chaplain at the moment. I just get so much encouragement from her, she just sees things as they really are.'

Some people obtained this kind of support through networks, for example based around their church tradition, specific support groups such as cell groups and counselling. Others found support from parish staff such as churchwardens, and parishioners. Spiritual support was also important to many of the participants.

Clergy colleagues were an important source of such support, as were spiritual directors. Some people identified that going on retreat helped them to obtain this kind of support.

Training offered by dioceses was identified as important for career development. Leadership development training was seen to be particularly useful, since it gave clergy skills and insights that they might not otherwise have developed, as a female priest in mid-career describes:

> 'Our diocese did a leadership course which was very helpful … my preferred style is not really upfront leadership, it's much more facilitating, enabling, but sometimes in my job I have to say well, this is where we're at, and there isn't any space for negotiation, and I really don't like doing that. The leadership course was very helpful on this.'

Some of the clergy interviewed had had 'successful' careers in other fields before they were ordained. They believed that their previous work experience had given them skills and expertise that were useful in a church context and therefore helped them in their church careers.

Conclusion

The research findings show that clergy have distinctive notions of career success, derived from their calling to the priesthood but also reflecting a desire for influence, development and recognition within the Church. While the conceptualizations of success identified are distinctive, some of them reflect career orientations and models of success identified in earlier studies, such as the lifestyle career anchor and Influencer and Expert definitions of career success.[14] It is important to note that the findings suggest that there may be more that the Church of England can do to facilitate clergy career development and satisfaction, especially in terms of career support, training, management and review. Affirmation and recognition of clergy achievements are also necessary if clergy are to feel successful and fulfilled in their work.

Notes

1. R. Christopherson, 'Calling and Career in Christian Ministry', *Review of Religious Research*, 35(3), 1994, pp. 219–237.

2. Christopherson, 'Calling and Career in Christian Ministry'.

3. J. Arnold, *Managing Careers in the Twenty-first Century*, London: Paul Chapman, 1997.

4. E. Schein, 'Career Anchors Revisited: Implications for Career Development in the Twenty-first Century', *Academy of Management Executive*, 10(4), 1996, pp. 80–88.

5. Schein, 'Career Anchors Revisited'; J. Sturges, 'What it Means to Succeed: Personal Conceptions of Career Success Held by Male and Female Managers at Different Ages', *British Journal of Management*, 10(3), 1999, pp. 239–252.

6. E. Schein, *Career Dynamics: Matching Individual and Organizational Needs*, Reading MA: Addison Wesley, 1978; Schein, 'Career Anchors Revisited'.

7. Schein, *Career Dynamics*.

8. Schein, 'Career Anchors Revisited'.

9. Sturges, 'What it Means to Succeed'.

10. A. Wrzesniewski, C. McCauley, P. Rosin and B. Schwartz, 'Jobs, Careers and Callings: People's Relations to Their Work', *Journal of Research in Personality*, 3, 1997, pp. 21–33.

11. D. T. Hall and D. Chandler, 'Psychological Success: When the Career is a Calling', *Journal of Organizational Behavior*, 26, 2005, pp. 155–176.

12. B. Dik and R. Duffy, 'Calling and Vocation at Work: Definitions and Prospects for Research and Practice', *The Counselling Psychologist*, 37(3), 2009, pp. 424–450.

13. Since this research was conducted each of the participating dioceses has systematically reviewed and is in the process of revising their Ministerial Development Review arrangements (Editor's note).

14. Schein, 'Career Anchors Revisited'; J. Sturges, 'What it Means to Succeed'.

5

'Still in Saigon?'
Ministry, Movies and Moving On

JUSTIN LEWIS-ANTHONY

Begin at the end

Picture this. You are in a completely darkened room, looking at a darkened screen. There is no noise, until, gradually, sound begins to sweep across the auditorium – helicopter blades, heavily processed. The darkness on the screen fades to grey, also gradually, and we see the edge of a jungle, flattened through the compression of a telephoto lens. A helicopter sweeps across the screen, smoke blows and, interpolated with more swishing blades, the raga-guitar figures of 'The End' play.[1] A moment before Jim Morrison sings the opening lines ('This is the end, beautiful friend'), the jungle erupts in an inferno of napalm, but we do not hear the noise of the explosion, just more helicopters and guitars. The camera begins to pan to the right as the smoke billows and multiple aircraft flick across our view. Overlaid, on the left of the screen, we see a man (Martin Sheen) in close-up. He is upside down, pensively smoking a cigarette. Another overlay image, a ceiling fan, echoes the blades of the choppers. Flames continue to rise, and an impassive carved face of an Indochinese temple deity is shown as a pendant to the smoking man. The music fades beneath the sound of a bass-heavy rhythmic beating; we are unsure whether it is a ceiling fan or a helicopter blade. The camera spins on the smoking man, until we see him sleeping in the detritus of a chaotic hotel room: 'all the children are insane'. All that is left is the (processed) sound of the ceiling fan, and gradually the man comes to, staggers from his bed, and looks, cautiously, through the blinds of his hotel room. There is a world outside: busy and lacking in explosions. We hear, in voiceover, his reaction: 'Saigon. S**t. I'm still only in Saigon.'

This is the opening scene of *Apocalypse Now*, by Francis Ford Coppola (Coppola 1979).[2] The film tells the story of Captain Willard (Martin Sheen), dispatched up the Nang river during the Vietnam war on a mission to find and execute a renegade US Army Colonel, Kurtz (Marlon Brando). To underline the madness that Willard finds along the river and at Kurtz's compound, Coppola begins the film with the destruction of the world. The Apocalypse in *Apocalypse Now* takes place in the film's first reel. It shows Coppola's profoundly pessimistic point of view: the journey begins with complete destruction, and, to be stuck in Saigon only means that Willard has the whole journey towards destruction to undertake (again!).

All very engrossing, and a memorable introduction to a memorable film. But is there something more to Willard's predicament, something we can apply to the task in hand? Can we say that there are parallels between the experience of Willard in the hotel room and a hypothetical parson in a parish, facing (a) transition(s) in ministry? Of course, the answer is 'Yes'.

As many spiritual writers have observed, not least among whom we may name C. S. Lewis and Thomas Merton, the sin of *accidia* (aka acedia, or despondency) can affect those whose vocation is externally focused in love and service. Lewis acknowledged his susceptibility to accidia (letter to Don Giovanni Calabria, 10 September 1949),[3] and described his many accomplishments as 'my lame defeats'.[4] In another letter (to Arthur Greeves, 10 February 1930) he described the effect of accidia as making its sufferer as an 'unstringed instrument', that is, useless for its purpose, and all the more mocking in its uselessness.[5] Merton, with his thorough grounding in the work of the desert fathers on accidia, knew what the sin looked like when translated into a twentieth-century church framework:

> The inertia of conventional religious life is like a deep sleep from which one only awakens from time to time, to realize how deeply he has been sleeping. Then he falls back into it.[6]

You wake up, find yourself still in Saigon, then fall back to sleep. How can cinema help us to reflect on this problem? In what ways can cinema address the issues of pastoral restlessness, human wilfulness, 'stuckness' in ministry, and psychological dis-ease of which accidia seems to be part? In order to answer that question we need to ask, simply, can cinema be theological?

The theology of film?

A 'common-sense' answer to this question would surely be 'No'. Theology is high-brow, cinema is low-brow. The Church is concerned with humanity's better nature, cinema panders to our baser instincts. That is the story which we are told and which we tell ourselves. Just think how closely 'churchgoer' and 'censorship' go together in the history of cinema.

Curiously enough, this was not the situation in the first 30 years of cinema's history. In May 1920 the anonymous author of *The Literary Digest*'s survey of the relationship between cinema and Church described how '"film sermons" now play an important role in the propagation of every-day religion'.[7] Some clergy went further:

> The motion-picture can and must be an instrument for Christ's teachings. Its power for good is just as great as its power for harm. That its first use was in the exploitation of human weaknesses in thousands of movie 'dramas' should not blind us to its use in the extension of the Kingdom. Guided and directed by Christian minds, the motion-picture is destined to become a powerful influence in the cause of Christianity and righteousness.[8]

The optimistic attitude soon soured, and with the sexual scandals in Hollywood in the early 1920s increasing pressure began to be exerted by the churches for censorship and control of the new art form's expression. Cinema, it came to be seen, was a royal road to depravity, a 'grave menace to youth, to home life, country and religion'.[9] James M. Wall provocatively summarized this attitude by asking: 'What has Jerusalem to do with Hollywood?'[10]

It was not until after the social turmoil of the Second World War, and the loosening of authoritarianism and the status of hierarchy in Western societies, that the exact opposite came to be asserted: Hollywood *was* Jerusalem. For some writers it was hard to distinguish between religion and film, for both aimed to bring their audience/congregation 'as close to the ineffable, invisible and unknowable as words, images and ideas' are able.[11] It was possible for cinema to 'usher us into the presence of the holy'.[12]

This way of thinking is based on the work of Rudolf Otto, who in the early twentieth century attempted to explore what we meant by 'holy'. When a human being encounters the holy, they become aware of their 'own nothingness in contrast to that which is supreme above all creatures'.[13] It is impossible to express this using words, arguments or reason. Men and women therefore describe such experiences through the use of 'metaphor and symbolic expressions'. Art and religions are examples of this use of metaphor and symbol.[14] In other words, when it comes to the important stuff, humanity is a metaphorical animal, and, moreover, one which likes its metaphors to have a beginning, a middle and an end. Our metaphors are stories.

Metaphors which are stories have a special name: we call them 'myths'. This is not another word for 'lie', or 'fairy tale'. Rather, a myth is a story we tell in order to make sense of our world and our lives. Myths are 'framing metaphors', by which we arrange 'raw nature, facts, data' into 'ruling stories'.[15] They help us to make sense of our experiences, as individuals and as a people.

The myths aren't always obviously identifiable as myths: not all myths begin with 'Once upon a time'! So, for example, as Kelton Cobb points out, the range of 'framing metaphors' of our time includes such myths as 'survival of the fittest, rational choice, secularization, globalization, the war of all against all, dialectical materialism, chaos theory, the cunning collusion of power and knowledge, the triumph of the therapeutic, the decline of civilization, the "end of history", the "clash of civilizations", the Big Bang and Murphy's Law'.[16] They gain in power by being ubiquitous, and camouflaged as 'just the way things are' or 'the real world'. According to Cobb, myths 'shape us secretly at a formative age and remain with us, informing the ongoing narrative constructions of our experience. They teach us how to perceive the world as we order our outlooks and choices in terms of their patterns and plots'.[17]

Film and myth

This sounds like a description of how film works on its audiences: we live in a visual age, where almost everyone is familiar with the stories, scripts and images of famous films and we can quote them and refer to them ('Use the force, Luke', 'He's not the messiah!', 'I'll be back', 'Frankly, my dear, I don't give a damn!', 'You talking to me?'). More than 30 years ago Paul Monaco described how cinema achieves this mythical status. It does so by appearing to look real, while at the same time it 'transcends reality (quasi-magically)'.[18] It looks real because it deals with visual images, things 'up there' on the screen: we are willing enough to believe that patterns of light show us 'real' objects and creatures (even if those creatures are Na'vi from Pandora). It is 'quasi-magical' because cinema can, for example, manipulate time, as we saw in the complicated chronological structure of the opening scenes of *Apocalypse Now*. Film-makers do this using a technique called 'parallel editing', so that the transitions in time are, or should be, invisible to the audience – see, for example, the most famous 'jump-cut' in cinematic history: the transition between prehistoric man throwing a thigh-bone into the air, and the orbiting space weapon system in *2001: A Space Odyssey*.[19]

Remember as well, that films are art-forms dependent on huge, and expensive, quantities of technology. They are a product of industrial capitalism, and therefore are almost never made by an individual: as Monaco says, 'Movies are not "authored" but are rather reflections of shared thoughts and structures ... [and such collective thinking is] impersonal, archetypic, and prototypic.'[20] In other words, cinema is a *shared* mythology: it tells us the stories we all think are important.

Theology and film and ministry?

How do we experience these stories? How are we exposed to them? Think about the (usual) way in which a film is experienced: we need to reflect on the difference between *seeing* and *watching*. As the secular film critic Tom Sutcliffe put it, the verb we use to describe our interaction (or otherwise) with a film indicates the nature of that interaction: '"seeing" is a word that usually implies a kind of passivity of reception ... [and] when used specifically of vision ... is a kind of lowest common denominator'.[21] Watching, on the other hand, brings 'a particular kind of scrutiny to bear on the screen'. It 'implies a narrowing of the field of vision', and, furthermore, 'contains a flavour of expectation, the sense of waiting for something to become manifest or change its nature'.[22] Furthermore, this is not a haphazard achievement, but, as Jann Cather Weaver says, 'is a disciplined task, not confined to the ocular function of sight'. Rather, to watch a film in this way is to practise 'the critical discipline of delving beneath surface'. It is to be 'intentional, participatory'.[23] And, in its theological manifestation, it has a moral component as well, for, as Jesus asked of the disciples, 'Do you have eyes, and fail to see?' (Mark 8.18, echoing Isa. 6.9–10 and Jer. 5.21).[24]

How do we watch films as a disciplined task? Part of the discipline will be to learn something of the art and techniques of film-making, to understand the 'grammar' of cinema. There are any number of books that will help you do that in a systematic and learned way: among the best are Bordwell and Thompson's *Film Art*, Hill and Gibson's *Oxford Guide to Film Studies* and, most completely, Barsam and Monahan's *Looking at Movies*, the 3rd edition of which, although expensive, includes two DVDs of film clips and examples.[25] If reading further or more deeply is not for you, then you may find useful the series of questions I worked on for a parish youth group film club. I invited the members of 'Light in the Dark' to ask themselves a series of questions as they watched any film, grouped into three sections: the movie itself, you as the spectator, and what the combination of the two might say about religion: film, viewer, faith, if you like.

First, film: How well put together is the film's story? Is there a 'story-arc'? Is it clear? If it isn't, is this a deliberate decision of the film-maker? How do the characters develop over the course of the film (if at all)? Is their development convincing? What are the actors' performances like? Is there a particularly powerful/moving performance? How does the actor achieve this?

Moving from the story and the performance to the technical aspects of the film we can ask how the film is photographed (its cinematography). Is it striking? Is there any significance to the colour palette used? How does the film use music, in the world of the film (technically 'diegetically'), or as a soundtrack (technically 'extra-diegetically[26])? Do you notice any striking use of camera angles or sequence cuts?

Recognizing that a film's effect depends upon its viewers, it is proper to ask, what is your first reaction to the film? What moves/repels/speaks to you? Of the characters in the story, which is most important for you? Is this the most important character for the film and film-maker?

Which leads us on to questions of faith. Does the film have a 'message'? What is it? Do you notice any overtly religious commentary/symbolism in the film? How is this used (sympathetically, antagonistically, part of the story, part of character development)? Can you see anything which challenges your understanding of God (theology), or your ideas about what is right and wrong (ethics)? What do your theology and ethics have to say about the characters in, and the story of, the film?

None of this has to be done as you are watching the film: suspension of disbelief is sometimes necessary to appreciate a film, and so is suspension of belief. If you are able to hold the questions in the back of your mind as you attend to the film, then you will find reflecting on the film after the viewing to be very rewarding. You will be able to articulate the reasons why you might have responded to the film in a particular way. In this way, it might be helpful to think of thinking theologically about film as a form of Ignatian Spiritual Exercise, a 'way of examining one's conscience, of meditating, of contemplating, of praying vocally and mentally, and of performing other spiritual actions …'.[27]

We will look at how these techniques of cinematic literacy can be applied to two recent films, *The Way* and *Of Gods and Men* (both 2010). Both films are good examples of films (that is, they are of a high cinematic quality), and they both illuminate our topic in complementary and contrasting ways.

The Way

Emilio Estevez's great achievement in *The Way* is to depict the connection between parental bereavement and moving on without succumbing to cloying sentimentality.[28] The film tells the story of Tom Avery, a settled, conservative and irascible ophthalmologist from Ventura, California, who travels reluctantly to St-Jean-Pied-de-Port in the French Pyrenees to repatriate the body of his only son. Daniel died in a mountain accident, one day into walking the Camino, the pilgrimage route which leads through the Pyrenees across northern Spain to the shrine of St James in Santiago de Compostela. Tom and Daniel were estranged; the father's complacency and the son's fecklessness equally to blame. The power of the relationship, which is related through flash-back, and present visions, is strengthened by the casting: Estevez plays Daniel, his real-life father, Martin Sheen plays Tom.

At first Tom's only intention is to retrieve his son's body and meagre possessions, and to return to California as soon as he can. However, on a whim, unexplainable to anyone, but especially to himself, he decides to take his son's ashes on the pilgrimage, and to walk the 500 miles to Santiago. He is an unprepared pilgrim. As the film's press kit says: Tom is 'reluctant, uncertain, skeptical, a bit broken and yet, for all his fierce independence, most definitely in need of sustenance from others on his way through'.[29]

Tom is shown to be comfortable in the company of his golfing companions in California, but following his son's death he knows, full well, that there is nothing to be gained from the company of others ('Do you think [Tom] would want to talk to me about it?' 'I think he'd sooner shove that walking stick down your throat'.) And yet, despite himself, he picks up companions: Joost (Yorick Van Wageningen), the 'fat Dutchman' who is walking to lose weight; Sarah (Deborah Kara Unger) from Canada who only wants to quit cigarettes; Jack (James Nesbitt), a writer from

Northern Ireland who is struggling with writer's block – Estevez has admitted the conscious allusion to Dorothy and her three companions in *The Wizard of Oz*.[30]

Tom knew what he would experience before he set off, and none of it would be worthwhile: 'We're all just taking a really long walk, I suppose'. His only aspiration is to walk the Camino, gradually divesting himself of his son's ashes. And yet, as Estevez wrote the part and Sheen played it, the key to understanding Tom is the 'chipping away slowly and subtly at the thick slabs of armor [he] has built around himself, as a father and as a man, over the years'.[31] Tom believes that the Camino, and the *peregrinos* he meets, have nothing that he needs. But, as Sheen put it, 'Over time, [Tom] begins to see that he's going to have to learn to rely on others – and more than that, he's going to have to let them know that they can rely on him.'[32]

Unusually for such texts, the press kit contains an epigraph, in Latin and ascribed to St Augustine: 'Solvitur ambulando' ('It is solved by walking'). Although this advice is often credited to Augustine of Hippo, it does not appear, to my knowledge, in the extant corpus of his writings. Handley Moule, evangelical churchman and later Bishop of Durham, in a discussion on the doctrine of election, opined *'solvitur ambulando cum Deo'*.[33] Estevez isn't so crude in his exploration of Tom's faith. Tom criticizes the easy comfort of his parish priest in California ('Would you like to pray with me Tom?' 'What for?'), receives a rosary from another American catholic priest he meets on the way ('There are a lot of lapsed Catholics out here on the camino, kid'), leaves a stone as a sign of his penitence at the Cruz de Ferro waypoint, and attends mass in the Cathedral in Santiago. But there is no conversion experience, and, if anything, for Tom the answer to the stuckness of his life comes with *solvitur ambulando cum filio*: the last shot is Tom, still with Daniel's jacket and rucksack walking through a casbah in Arab north Africa. Captain Willard has moved from Saigon, through suburban California, into northern Spain and the rest of the world. Going for a really long walk, in the company of others, has allowed him to break out of the prison of circumstances and attitude.

Of Gods and Men

Tom Avery finishes his journey of liberation where our next film begins. *Of Gods and Men*[34] tells the story of eight French Christian monks who live in a monastery in the remote Atlas mountains of Algeria. It is closely based on the life and death of the Cistercian monks of Our Lady of Atlas, near the village of Tibhirine, under the inspired witness of their Abbot, Dom Christian de Chergé (played by Lambert Wilson).

The film begins with an almost directionless depiction of the rhythm of the monks' life: praying, singing, working their fields, making honey. The monks read and write letters for their illiterate neighbours, and participate in the village's rites of passage. Br Luc (Michel Lonsdale) runs a free medical clinic. But in the 1990s, as Islamist fundamentalism begins to find violent expression, the monks realize that their monastery, their way of life and their relationships with the (Muslim) villagers who live clustered around the monastery, are all threatened. The situation worsens when a construction crew of European workers are brutally killed nearby. Caught between the threat of the insurgents and the offers of 'protection' from the Algerian Army, the monks are uncertain about their future and their vocation. Should they leave? What would that say to the villagers? What good can be achieved by remaining, when it is made clear to them by both government and terrorists that they are remnants of French colonial power? As the village elders say to them: 'We're the birds. You're the branch. If you go, we lose our footing.'

The decision to stay is not an easy one. At a chapter meeting Br Christophe (Olivier Rabourdin) asks:

And if they come here? We lie down and die?
[Christian] It's a risk, yes. We were called to live here, in this country, with these people, who are also afraid. We'll live with this unknown, yes.
[Christophe] I didn't come here to commit collective suicide.
[Luc] Perhaps we could determine what each of us could do if they came here?
[Christophe] What is there to do?
[Luc, mischievously] Play hide-and-seek?

Christophe experiences a crisis of faith and vocation. His prayers at night are noisy and violent, like Jacob wrestling with the angel of his fears. He speaks to Dom Christian:

[Christophe] Dying, here and now, does it achieve anything?
[Christian] Remember. You've already given your life. You gave it by following Christ. When you decided to leave everything. Your life, your family, your country. The family you could have raised.
[Christophe] I don't know if it's true anymore. I don't get it. Why be martyrs? For God? To be heroes? To prove we're the best?

There is no easy solution, no argument into conviction or courage. Rather Christophe *and* Christian continue to live in their fears and their uncertainties within the community. We see what this means in one of the most moving scenes of the film. It begins with a shot from the deck of a helicopter gunship, flying low over the tumble-down village. There is no extra-diegetic music (no *Ride of the Valkyries* to add pomp and menace). We cut to the interior of the monastery chapel, looking down on the monks gathered in silent meditation before the midday office. They, and we, can hear the thump of the rotor blades. We cut to the point of view of the helicopter: this time the machine gun is pointing directly at the chapel. Dom Christian stands, in consternation. The sound of the helicopter is oppressive; overwhelming. Christian begins to sing, and the other monks stand and join him: 'O Father of light, Eternal light, And source of all light. You illuminate us, at the threshold of night, With the radiance of your face.' It is an evening hymn (based upon Psalms 134, 139, 141), even though the day is bright outside. As they sing we see the helicopter hovering, at tree height, threatening the monastery by its presence and its noise. We cut to the interior of the chapel, but now a shoulder height point of view, behind the monks, looking up through the east window towards the source of the noise and threat. Gradually, extra-diegetically, the sound of the helicopter fades away and the 'Amen' of the monks' hymn remains, defiant.

The monks decide to stay, together. Following the decision, they eat the evening meal, and Br Luc, mischievously, and without permission, plays a recording of Tchaikovsky. It is the only recorded music in the film, and as *Swan Lake* plays, Beauvois shows us the faces of the monks, caught up in the beauty of the music, and the solemnity of their decision.

But it was not *Swan Lake* that gave the monks the moral strength to face and accept their death. Rather, it was by being religious, living under a rule and within a creedal order, which allowed them to face their greatest fear. The Trappists show that sometimes, being religious gives people more than our society thinks can be possible.

They are taken, in the night, by the insurgents, imprisoned and beaten. Over a montage of snow on the deserted monastery, its cemetery, the frozen cloister, the empty chapter room, we hear Dom Christian reading his final testament.

> If the day comes, and it could be today, that I am a victim of the terrorism that seems to be engulfing all foreigners living in Algeria, I would like my community, my Church, and my family, to remember that I have dedicated my life to God and Algeria.[35]

He addresses his future killer, in words that show the true Christian compassion and witness of this twentieth-century martyr:

> And to you, too, my friend of the last moment, who will not know what you are doing. Yes, for you, too, I wish this thank-you and this 'A-Dieu', whose image is in you also, that we may meet in heaven, like happy thieves, if it pleases God, our common Father. Amen! Inshallah![36]

The final scene shows the monks being marched by their captors through the thick snow and fog of an Atlas winter. Gradually they all disappear into white.

Santiago, Saigon and Tibhirine

By 1929 H. G. Wells had already recognized that the production-line that churned out the screenplays for popular cinema was a symbiosis of myth and capitalism: the 'themes, the concepts, the methods that ruled in popular fiction, popular drama and the music-hall were transferred to the cinemas copiously and profitably, and with the greatest possible economy of adaptation'.[37] What was true in 1929 remains true today.[38] The reason why *The Way* and *Of Gods and Men* can be used for a reflective theological engagement is not because they are superficially films with 'religious' themes (pilgrimage! monks!), but because their makers wish to honour something that is ambivalent, polyvalent, within human experience, and which, furthermore, doesn't need spelling out. The films recognize, in the words of Roger Ebert, that there are some problems deeper than 'the characters have not slept with each other', and their solution(s) are more complex and intractable than 'they do'.[39] In *The Way* Tom's problem is that he is trapped, and he doesn't realize it. In *Of God's and Men*, the monks' problem is that they are trapped and they do realize it.

For Tom, through moving, and opening himself up to the rough irritations of other people, he realizes his liberation. For the monks, through remaining still, in stability and in community, and opening themselves up to the reality of the promise they had already made, they have their liberation realized for them. As Br Luc puts it in a conversation with Dom Christian: 'I'm not scared of terrorists, even less of the army. And I'm not scared of death. I'm a free man.'

Tom progresses and transforms. He realizes that it isn't just a really long walk he's been on, and the kilometerage is the least significant part of his journey.

The monks abide and are transformed. They realize that the place to which they were called remains the place to which they are called, even in the face of (worldly) failure and destruction. Early in the film we are shown a meal in which the lection prefigures the monk's fate:

> Accepting our powerlessness and our extreme poverty is an invitation, an urgent appeal to create with others relationships not based on power. Recognizing my weaknesses, I accept those of others. I can bear them, make them mine in imitation of Christ. Such an attitude transforms us for our mission. Weakness in

itself is not a virtue, but the expression of a fundamental reality which must constantly be refashioned by faith, hope and love.[40]

This can stand as a gloss for the journeys of both the monks and ophthalmologist. As protagonists in films, a mythic art-form, Tom and the monks reflect on their situations. The means by which they do this, and the answers they come up with, are very different, but the processes and the conclusions are reasonable depictions of the things that our society (whether the professional bourgeoisie of California or the professional religious of North Africa) values. The film-makers take, and reflect back to us, the world in which we live.

Seeing the world reflected in cinematic art, and understanding how that reflection works, can both reassure and challenge those ministers of the church who wish to reflect upon their own vocations. Ask yourself the questions about how the film-makers have made their films. Ask yourself about the decisions the protagonists made. Ask yourself what is valued in the films and what you value in your own ministry and vocation. Then decide where you need to be.

Notes

1. The Doors, *The End*, Elektra Records, 1967.

2. Francis Ford Coppola, *Apocalypse Now*, Technovision/Technicolor. USA: United Artists, 1979.

3. Letter to Don Giovanni Calabria, 10 September 1949, C. S. Lewis, *Yours, Jack: Spiritual Direction from C. S. Lewis*, ed. Paul F. Ford, London: HarperOne, 2008.

4. 'The Apologist's Evening Prayer', C. S. Lewis, *The Collected Poems of C. S. Lewis*, ed. Walter Hooper, 2nd edn, London: Fount Paperbacks, 1994.

5. Lewis, *Yours, Jack*, p. 11.

6. Letter to Ernesto Cardenal, 18 November 1959, Thomas Merton, *Courage For Truth: The Letters of Thomas Merton to Writers*, ed. Christine M. Bochen, *The Thomas Merton Letters* 4, New York: Harcourt, Brace, 1994, p. 120.

7. Anon., 'The Motion-Picture as a "Handmaid of Religion"', *The Literary Digest*, 15 May 1920, p. 46.

8. The Revd Paul Smith of the Episcopalian Church, quoted in 'The

Motion-Picture as a "Handmaid of Religion"', p. 47. For two good overviews of the first 40 years of the Church's relationship with cinema see Terry Lindvall, 'Silent Cinema and Religion: An Overview (1895–1930)' and Andrew Quicke, 'The Era of Censorship (1930–1967)' in *The Routledge Companion to Religion and Film*, ed. John Lyden, London: Routledge, 2009, pp. 13–31 and 31–51.

9. James M. Skinner, *The Cross and the Cinema: The Legion of Decency and the National Catholic Office for Motion Pictures, 1933–1970*, Westport CT; London: Praeger, 1993, p. 38.

10. James M. Wall, *Church and Cinema: A Way of Viewing Film*, Grand Rapids MI: Eerdmans, 1971, chapter 1.

11. Paul Schrader, *Transcendental Style in Film: Ozu, Bresson, Dreyer*, Berkeley, CA: University of California Press, 1972, p. 8.

12. Robert K. Johnston, *Reel Spirituality: Theology and Film in Dialogue*, Grand Rapids MI: Baker Books, 2000, p. 118.

13. Rudolf Otto, *The Idea of the Holy: An Inquiry into the Non-Rational Factor in the Idea of the Divine and Its Relation to the Rational*, Oxford: Oxford University Press, 1923, p. 10.

14. Otto, *The Idea of the Holy*, p. 12.

15. William G. Doty, *Mythography: The Study of Myths and Rituals*, University, AL: University of Alabama Press, 1986, p. 18.

16. Kelton Cobb, *The Blackwell Guide to Theology and Popular Culture*, Blackwell Guides to Theology, Oxford: Blackwell Publishing, 2005, pp. 123–124.

17. Cobb, *Blackwell Guide*, p. 123.

18. Paul Monaco, 'Film as Myth and National Folklore', in *The Power of Myth in Literature and Film: Selected Papers from the Second Annual Florida State University Conference on Literature and Film*, ed. Victor Carrabino, pp. 35–49, Tallahassee: University Presses of Florida, 1980, p. 37.

19. Stanley Kubrick, *2001: A Space Odyssey*, Super Panavision 70 mm, UK/USA: Metro-Goldwyn-Mayer, 1968.

20. Monaco, 'Film as Myth and National Folklore', p. 39.

21. Tom Sutcliffe, *Watching: Reflections On the Movies*, London: Faber and Faber, 2000, pp. xiii–xiv.

22. Sutcliffe, *Watching*, pp. xiii, xiv.

23. Jann Cather Weaver, 'Discerning the Religious Dimensions of Film: Toward a Visual Method Applied to "Dead Man Walking"', presented at the Conference of American Academy of Religion, New Orleans, November 1996, quoted in Conrad E. Ostwalt, 'Teaching Religion and Film: A Fourth Approach', in *Teaching Religion and Film*, ed. Gregory J. Watkins, pp. 35–57, AAR Teaching Religious Studies, Oxford: Oxford University Press, 2008, p. 37.

24. There is an enormous field which deals with questions of visual culture and a much smaller one which is beginning to take seriously the

relationship between theology and visual studies. Among the former see Jane Kromm and Susan Benforado Bakewell (eds), *A History of Visual Culture: Western Civilization from the 18th to the 21st Century*, Oxford; New York: Berg, 2010; Margarita Dikovitskaya, *Visual Culture: The Study of the Visual After the Cultural Turn*, Cambridge MA: MIT Press, 2005; James Elkins, *Visual Studies: A Skeptical Introduction*. New York; London: Routledge, 2003; among the latter Stewart M. Hoover, *Religion in the Media Age, Religion, Media and Culture*, London: Routledge, 2006; Christopher Deacy and Elisabeth Arweck (eds), *Exploring Religion and the Sacred in a Media Age*, Theology and Religion in Interdisciplinary Perspective Series in Association with the BSA Sociology of Religion Study Group, Ashgate, 2009; Stephen Pattison, *Seeing Things: Deepening Relations with Visual Artefacts*, The Gifford Lectures, 2007, London: SCM Press, 2007.

25. David Bordwell and Kristin Thompson, *Film Art: An Introduction*, 9th edn, New York: McGraw-Hill, 2010; John Hill and Pamela Church Gibson (eds), *The Oxford Guide to Film Studies*, Oxford: Oxford University Press, 1998; Richard Meran Barsam and Dave Monahan, *Looking at Movies: An Introduction to Film*, 3rd edn, New York: W. W. Norton, 2010.

26. The Doors' song in *Apocalypse Now* is extra-diegetic; the noise of the Saigon street is diegetic.

27. St Ignatius of Loyola, *Spiritual Exercises*, trans. Elder Mullan, SJ, Raleigh NC: Hayes Barton Press, 2009, annotation 1.

28. Emilio Estevez, *The Way*, Technicolor/Super 16, USA Icon Entertainment International, 2010.

29. Robyn Leff, 'Press Kit for "The Way"', Métropole Films Distribution, 2010; www.metropolefilms.com.

30. Victor Fleming, *The Wizard of Oz*, 35 mm Technicolor Three-Strip, USA: Metro-Goldwyn-Mayer, 1939.

31. Leff, 'Press Kit', p. 7.

32. Leff, 'Press Kit', p. 7.

33. H. C. G. Moule, *Outlines of Christian Doctrine*, 3rd edn, London: Hodder and Stoughton, 1890, p. 47.

34. Xavier Beauvois, *Of Gods and Men*, Techniscope/35 mm, France: Artificial Eye, 2010.

35. John W. Kiser, *The Monks of Tibhirine: Faith, Love, and Terror in Algeria*, New York: St Martin's Griffin, 2003, p. 244. Kiser's translation differs slightly from the subtitles in the film. There is another English translation available in Donald McGlynn's summary of the events at Tibhirine (Donald McGlynn, 'Atlas Martyrs', *Cistercian Studies* 32(2), 1997. pp. 149–194, [pp. 188–189]).

36. Kiser, *The Monks of Tibhirine*, p. 246.

37. H. G. Wells, 'The Film, the Art Form of the Future (1929)', in *Meanwhile, the Picture of a Lady; and the King Who Was a King*, London: Waterlow & Sons, 1933, pp. 177–181.

38. Excepting, perhaps, any injunction to economy: c.f. *Avatar* and *John Carter*, with estimated budgets of $237 million and $250 million respectively (James Cameron, *Avatar*, DeLuxe/35mm/70mm/IMAX, USA: Twentieth Century-Fox Film Corporation, 2009; Andrew Stanton, *John Carter*, DeLuxe/35mm/70mm/IMAX, USA: Walt Disney Studios Motion Pictures, 2012.

39. Roger Ebert, '"Station Agent" Finds Depth Beyond Comedy, Sadness', *Chicago Sun-Times*, 17 October, sec. Weekend Plus, 2003.

40. The reading is not identified in the film, but it comes from a sermon preached by Fr Christian Chessel, 'In My Weakness, I Find My Strength'. A longer extract is quoted by Kiser (*The Monks of Tibhirine*, p. 199). Chessel was murdered in Tizi-Ouzou in December 1994.

6

A Pilgrimage to My Own Self?
R. S. Thomas and the Poetic Character
of Reflective Ministry

MARK PRYCE

How do we do justice to the creativity of messy ministry?

An unintended consequence of well-meant counsels of perfection is to breed a sense of failure. Handbooks for professionals have their dangers. Those who feel themselves not to be living up to expectations may become despondent. Ideals can inhibit – or worse, foster neuroses, like exquisite size-zero fashion models inspiring bulimia in vulnerable adolescents. Guides to healthy living can evoke hypochondria – a plague of anxiety among the 'worried well'. As other contributors in this collection argue, ministers need appropriate training and formation, a framework for accountability that sustains a sense of purpose in our work, regular reflection-on-practice and ministerial review, and a direction of travel with criteria for measuring achievement accompanied by resources for personal and professional development. All these are good and necessary. Yet will they sort out messiness and imperfection or erase dissatisfaction from clergy lives? Will better-managed transitions guarantee solutions to life's untidiness? Will role descriptions and well-conducted MDRs bring vocational resolution at each and every point? Is there any place for ministerial uncertainty? How might it be appreciated as a source of wisdom, or even as the fruits of holiness?

While the security of Common Tenure requires a certain degree of compliance from those who benefit, clergy also need a place in which we may continue to give room to the struggle, wrestle with and even entertain a little hesitancy about the task and identity of the ordained priest. Such ministerial unease can be creative, generative of new understandings and directions. Indeed, we may not have a choice but to find such a space if the Church wants human beings in public representative ministry rather than operatives of a system. People are messy, and perhaps a messy Church in a messy world needs messy priests? I do not mean chaotic or destructive clergy, but those who have a sense of their own unease or unresolvedness in ministry and are committed to working with this as a dimension of ministerial experience that can yield valuable insights and motivations for human flourishing.

It may be that the invitation to re-imagine ministry implies space for clergy to play host to the disruptive, speculative, searching and insatiable dimensions of imagination as they reflect on ministry. What, where and in whom are the resources and models for a more venturesome, less immediately conventional approach to ministerial development? Perhaps we need to learn from priests of the imagination, such as poets, who do not expect to practise the arts of their particular creativity through strategic processes that leave them comfortable, settled and secure in a list of objectives for the annual work schedule. What alternative models of critical, creative ministry are on offer?

Speaking from the edge: marginality in poetry and priesthood

One such is the Anglican priest-poet Ronald Stuart Thomas (1913–2000). This chapter takes two forms of writing – his poems and his autobiography – and interprets these literary works as written reflections on ministry. While the work of R. S. Thomas is by no means universally known and read, it seems that his poetic voice continues to find a significant and persistent audience among clergy and lay people in the churches and beyond. This is partly because R. S. Thomas (RS) writes as a poet who explores the experience of prayer and Christian spirituality in exceptionally perceptive, nuanced and evocative ways; but also, perhaps, because he writes as a priest-poet from a place which is marginal theologically, culturally and geographically. It is the insights which arise from R. S. Thomas's liminality which resonate with many of his readers, not least those who are ordained. The clarity, honesty and commitment he brings as a praying poet to the difficulty of sustaining an authentic spiritual ecology in which public ministry and personal discipleship can flourish, is both searing and inspiring. The felt isolation of ministry, or the discomfort he feels with his contemporary culture, or his resistance to the corporate trends he perceives in his Church, may be aspects of Thomas's writing which also connect with clergy who sense, in different circumstances, that the divine cannot be tamed by the institutional Church, nor adequately described by its theological codes or liturgical language. Indeed, in the poems the hidden yet incarnate God cannot be easily known or fluently described even in the powerful intimacy of human experience, and encountering this spiritual reality does not make for smug vicars or humorous poets. The bleakness of the poems arises from an interior landscape as well as the wet hill-country in which RS undertook his pastoral ministry.

Born and brought up in an English-speaking Welsh family, R. S. Thomas is widely acknowledged as one of the leading poets of modern Wales. Though his poetry is written exclusively in English, Wales and its people, culture, natural life and landscape are the constant subjects through which he explores universal themes of human identity and our relationship with the environment, technology and God. He was awarded the Queen's Gold Medal for Poetry in 1964, and nominated for the 1996 Nobel Prize in Literature. R. S. Thomas's literary work, particularly his poems, is written from his perspective as a priest, and this (not untroubled) viewpoint shapes his poetry of place and his nature poems as much as the more explicitly religious verse.

Ordained deacon in 1936, aged 23, and priest in 1937, from his earliest years as an ordained minister through to the final years of his life, R. S. Thomas wrote and published poems. Most of these poems arise out of his experience of ministry; they describe and also shape his practice and identity as a priest within the Church in Wales. The poems articulate R. S. Thomas's spirituality in an intimate yet public way, giving us access to the priest as a person of prayer who engages at a profound level with the pastoral issues he encounters, revealing the theological problems with which he wrestles, and charting the range of spiritual experience he embraces. His poems on Christian theology and spirituality are profound expressions of the struggle for faithfulness and intellectual integrity in a scientific, technological age. As such, the poems offer an exceptional insight into one priest's experience of over 40 years of full-time stipendiary ministry in the second half of the twentieth century, a ministry located entirely in the rural communities of mid and north Wales.

In contrast to this continuous lifelong stream of poetic reflection, R. S. Thomas's autobiography *Neb* speaks from the perspective of retirement as the priest looks back over his life and ministry. It was written in Welsh and first published in 1985, when RS was 72, with an English translation 12 years later. This retrospective overview enables R. S. Thomas to articulate a broad sense of the direction of travel which he feels himself to have taken across his life – his childhood, youth and formal education, his years of ministry and retirement, and the tenor of personal and professional relationships across that span. Yet as a ministerial autobiography *Neb* is no mere itinerary or reminiscence, but the intentional shaping of a personal, priestly story in a creative and self-critical way that generates fresh meaning and insight, opening up new questions and identifying challenges which remain unresolved for both the author and his readers. *Neb* is anything but a tidy or complacent story! As he describes the inner motivations and outer opportunities and constraints that have shaped his ministry and his poetic art, R. S. Thomas continues to find fresh perceptions and insights into the practice of ministry and its impact on the creative imagination and on the personal and spiritual life of the priest.

Words that move us on in ministry: poetic metaphors for priesthood

In making a brief survey of these two modes of ministerial reflection, poetry and autobiography, spanning a lifetime of service and a substantial period of his retirement, I will draw particular attention to the insights that R. S. Thomas offers in relation to his development as a priest. This will include attention to his development as a poet and man of prayer, because for RS these were integral to his priestly ministry. More specifically, I will identify the wisdom he distils in his reflections on times of transition from one phase of ministry to another, focusing his insights into ministry through five metaphors which evoke the reflective discipline that R. S. Thomas models in his written work: the priest as Pilgrim, as Steward, as Sentinel, as Fugitive and as Astronaut. The terms pilgrim and astronaut RS uses in his writing with reference to ministry. The Ordinal's language of steward and of sentinel find a richer and more nuanced tenor in the context of RS's personal and very particular reflections, an example of how the ordinary liturgical text and the extraordinary 'human document' of an inimitable lived life may illuminate and interpret one another. The term fugitive is used by the critic Justin Wintle to describe a particular transition in the poet's life, but I take it up as a kind of litmus to ask in what ways the theme of fleeing and escape might characterize the whole of R. S. Thomas's ministry, and whether there is a dimension of flight more generally in the apostolic task of ministerial priesthood. Indeed, though I focus on a particular metaphor at a certain stage in R. S. Thomas's life, I do so only to give emphasis to a particular dimension of his ministry which seems to emerge more strongly at that time or in that place. I am not suggesting a progression or succession from one to another.

As a whole the character of R. S. Thomas's reflective approach to ministry is *poetic* in the sense that it is a conscious and intentional making and constructing of a personal and priestly identity which is creative, interpretative, self-critical, speculative, evolving, cumulative and nuanced – and in this sense R. S. Thomas's poetic reflections through his poems and autobiography serve as a resource for contemporary ministers and their conversation partners who want to reflect on their own development in ways which foster creativity and insight, without shying away from a sense of uncertainty, difficulty or ambiguity as constructive sources of meaning and purpose.

Fostering a sense of journey in ministry: the priest as Pilgrim

Towards the end of his autobiography R. S. Thomas writes:

> Life is a pilgrimage, and if we have not succeeded in coming a little nearer to the truth, if we do not have a better comprehension of the nature of God before reaching the end of the journey, why was it that we started on the journey at all?[1]

This sentence suggests a certain sense of progression in his life's trajectory, a confidence that if we, as disciples and as priests, travel through our years also as pilgrims, then we will find enlightenment and fulfilment in and through the journey. Our experience as travellers yields wisdom and insight if we set out searching for these riches in an intentional way, moving on appreciatively with eyes wide open, taking time and making inner space to scan the distance we have come, rather than beetling ahead with our heads down tracking the next step one after another in a programmatic way. In writing his autobiography R. S. Thomas offers a positive vision of reflectiveness in ministry and discipleship.

Yet the title he gives his autobiography, *Neb*, translates in English as 'No one', and the life's pilgrimage he traces – though saturated with self-knowledge and profound insight – does not reach its end in a mood of calm fulfilment or sense of completeness. The story he tells is of a creative task that is always unfinished business. Looking back, R. S. Thomas describes the self he sees as 'no one' because the person he sees is a man always searching for himself without reaching resolution. The self is not a single, coherent entity which is consistently harmonious if only he can find 'the right place' or position in which to achieve ultimate satisfaction, as if the person, parson and poet will flourish only in the absence of difficulty. The poem 'Pilgrimages', published when RS was in his sixties, maps an ongoing journey into God, into self:

> ... Was the pilgrimage
> I made to come to my own
> self, to learn that in times
> like these and for one like me
> God will never be plain and
> out there, but dark rather and
> inexplicable, as though he were in here?[2]

The priest as pilgrim engages in a form of *poesis* – a meaning-making enterprise which requires a commitment to continual moving-on in understanding and the search for insight as s/he becomes more conscious of the challenges, problems, joys and opportunities that life and ministry present. In this sense, to write a narrative of purposeful journey and pilgrimage is not to smooth out the wrinkles in an untidy life and find a coherence which puts ministerial experience into some kind of harmonious sequence. As we shall see, to a great degree *Neb* might be characterized as the story of serial dissatisfactions and restlessness. R. S. Thomas moves from place to place, reaching after ideals and pursuing inner convictions, finding at each transition that he must adjust to the reality of actual circumstances in ministry. This inner trans-formation may be an occasion for learning, changed practice, and even for a deeper encounter with the mystery of God, though seldom a method for solving life's intractable difficulties. Indeed, we shall see that, in R. S. Thomas's understanding, the tensions and contradictions of ministry and personal life are not necessarily obstacles to a fulfilling life, but may even be the source and well-spring of creative art, flourishing ministry and spiritual wisdom if we choose to engage with them rather than evade them. Faithful ministry imagined as pilgrimage does not imply an easy journey, nor even a journey which brings an immediate sense of satisfac-tion, but a way of travelling in which the pilgrim engages at the deepest level with the people and the territory s/he encounters on the way, and seeks to serve faithfully in the situations that present themselves, and to learn from these occasions and encounters.

Such insight is not distilled instantaneously; it comes through a continual discipline of reflection on experience, developing awareness of self through constructing narratives of meaning, and becoming aware of how we create and refine these narratives in the light of experience as we go along, an awareness of our meaning-making processes which is self-critical and reflexive.

The early years of ministry in Chirk (1936–40) and Hanmer (1940–42): the priest as Steward

R. S. Thomas served his curacy in the parish of Chirk, where England meets the foothills of Wales. In *Neb* he remembers the first four years of ministry as a time of learning and encounter, but also as a period of frustration and dissatisfaction – like every curacy, perhaps! In visiting sick and elderly parishioners, particularly in the poorer coal-mining districts of the parish, he first encounters the suffering and loneliness of chronic ill-health, old age and deprivation of those inter-war years, and recognizes the solace that a faithful priest can bring simply by visiting regularly, bringing the sacrament and keeping company with isolated individuals. He learns what it is to be a steward of the mysteries of Christ as sacramental minister and pastor. At the same time he learns also to value the faith and courage of these individuals: they enrich the priest through their strength of character and generous appreciation of his ministry, and their suffering stewards him. Looking back over his ministry many years later, the experienced priest who first encounters 'the housebound' in Chirk sees what a stability they have sustained in him:

They keep me sober,
the old ladies
stiff in their beds,
mostly with pale eyes
wintering me ...
... Some fumble
with thick tongue for words,
and are deaf;

shouting their names
I listen;
they are far off,
the echoes return slow.

But without them,
without the subdued light
their smiles kindle,
I would have gone wild,
drinking earth's huge draughts
of joy and woe.[3]

As Chaplain of Toc H, an organization for ex-servicemen, he finds an opportunity to teach adults about literature, art and theology, fostering ethical debates about economics and world peace. In these unglamorous commitments the young priest learns what it is to be a steward of wisdom too – helping others to find insight and strength for their difficult lives through a faithful ministry of respectful pastoring and teaching and learning himself how to account for the mutual enrichment that takes place between priest and people. Ordination is much more than a mandate to serve others; it is an opportunity for the priest to grow and deepen as a person, disciple and scholar if he will take the trouble to move beyond accumulating skills and completing tasks into a deeper sense of how he is being changed through the role and formed by the community.

This is not to suggest that the early years of ministry are unfettered fulfilment: the young priest must learn to steward his own sense of vocation – to measure out his enthusiasms and passions and commitments within the confines of ecclesial structures which are not his to control. He must learn the obedience and discretion of a servant in the household where he is not master. This is painful and constraining. For example, when RS shares his pacifist inclinations from the pulpit, he is quickly silenced by the vicar, for whom ministry is about maintaining the careful theological and financial economy of the congregation, and working within the established power-dynamics of the given community that makes up Church, rather than disturbing the sincere convictions of others, let alone interpreting too literally the teachings of Jesus of Nazareth!

Chirk offered RS a different fulfilment: here he meets the sophisticated and well-travelled young English artist M. E. Eldridge (Elsie) who is to become his wife. Elsie encourages him in his enthusiasm for learning and in writing his first poems, a few of which are published in literary magazines. Together they drive up into the Welsh hills regularly and enjoy the beauty of nature. The young priest finds himself longing to escape – to speak Welsh and to spend more time in the remoter country of Wales, in the mountains which rise up to the west of Chirk, to return to the wild sea of his childhood home on Anglesey. In his autobiography RS gives this restlessness a retrospective cultural identity – *hiraeth* – the ancient Welsh term for the yearning in the heart of exiles longing to return to their Welsh homeland. As soon as he and Elsie marry they move to the parish of Hanmer on the western edge of the Cheshire plain, where RS is curate in charge of a district church, Tallarn Green. It is here that he and Elsie spend the first few years of the Second World War, witnessing the terrible bombing of Merseyside from a situation of relative safety. But this is not the right place for R. S. Thomas the Christian pacifist and poet. Though a conscientious parish priest, RS finds himself merely tolerating the flat farmland and the predominance of English culture. He learns that to be a steward is to have a responsibility to the inward convictions of vocation as well as to the outward expressions of worship, teaching, pastoral care and mission. He must steward himself as well as his parish, and as he listens to himself he hears a more intense yearning for a Welsh-speaking parish in the hills further west, to which he must respond; and he begins to learn Welsh in preparation for this ministry.

Rector of Manafon (1942–54): the priest as Sentinel

Manafon is just such a place: a parish in the heart of Montgomeryshire hill country where his parishioners are mainly Welsh farming families making a precarious living on their isolated hill-farms. It is the kind of context in which RS feels deeply that his ministry as a priest can flourish, and he serves 12 years here as parish priest: visiting regularly, teaching in the local school, maintaining regular services and preaching careful sermons which take their illustrations from nature and from farming. He and Elsie become parents of their only child, Gwydion. He continues to study, to learn Welsh, and to write his poems, publishing his first collections with small local presses. He writes as a kind of spy in the place, a watchman, a sentinel in the territory that is his to observe and to guard, as if his role is to name the life of the parish and its people. His poetry flourishes as he reflects on the bleak lives of his farmer-parishioners, finding in their 'peasant' lives a metaphor for the perennial human struggle with the forces of nature, inner and outer. He writes of Iago Prytherch, the archetypal farmer, trying as a poet to gauge him as a cautious watchman might, assessing his motives and his intentions, getting a feel for how best to communicate with him and reach him spiritually, elicit some kind of response out of his inscrutable nonchalance.

Though RS is ministering in what ought to be his ideal kind of parish, at a generous pace with a steady, dedicated rhythm which entirely suits him, what emerges in the poems is unease with the role and an inner sense of conflict with the people and the place, which seem so unyielding. In the poem 'A Priest to His People' the parson fumes:

> Men of the hills, wantoners, men of Wales,
> With your sheep and your pigs and your ponies, your sweaty
>   females,
> How I have hated you for your irreverence, your scorn even
> Of the refinements of art and the mysteries of the Church.
> I whose invective would spurt like a flame of fire
> To be quenched always in the coldness of your stare …
> … But I know as I listen that your speech has in it
> The source of all poetry, clear as a rill
> Bubbling from your lips; and what brushwork could equal
> The artistry of your dwelling on the bare hill?[4]

Though he has longed to minister among the Welsh-speaking Welsh in their native hills, what he perceives in this ideal location is a resistance to the things of the spirit and to beauty, culture and art: the Sentinel sees himself at risk in such a situation, he sees the souls of his parishioners at risk, and yet he cannot fail to acknowledge at the same time the profound poetry of the native speech and the artistry of their way of life as they make a living out of the difficult hill-country. Later he was to write as if the parish priest is a kind of sentry keeping watch over himself in an alien territory:

> I was vicar of large things
> in a small parish. Small-minded
> I will not say, there were depths
> in some of them I shrank back
> from, wells that the word 'God'
> fell into and died away,
> and for all I know is still
> falling ...
>   ... Often,
> when I thought they were about
> to unbar me, the draught
> out of their empty places
> came whistling, so that I wrapped
> myself in the heavier clothing
> of my calling, speaking of light and love
> in the thickening shadows of their kitchens.[5]

Vicar of Eglwysfach (1954–67): the priest as Fugitive

Tracing R. S. Thomas's move from Tallarn Green to Manafon, Justin Wintle describes him as a 'fugitive' priest.[6] RS was seeking a place in which he could think and write freely in accordance with his heart and his conscience, moving into a more yielding natural terrain and cultural environment. The same deep, inward shift is apparent in his move further westwards from Manafon to the parish of Eglwysfach, on the Dovey estuary. As a priest and a poet he was responding to an inner conviction, expecting that Eglwysfach will be a more creative place to work because of proximity to the sea and mountains, an area with exceptional bird-watching and wildlife, set in a Welsh-speaking area and close to the Welsh cultural centre of Aberystwyth. In *Neb* RS reflects on what he found in Eglwysfach: a village dominated by a boys' boarding school and a few assertive English families. As vicar RS feels pursued by excessive demands for conventional liturgy and music, conservative teaching and preaching. RS loathes the imperialist ethos which he feels the English expect their 'chaplain' to maintain – an uncritical patriotism and militarism to bolster the self-importance of retired men. 'The smell of the farmyard was replaced by the smell of the decayed conscience' he says sourly of his move from the Welsh farmers of Manafon to the retired army officers of Eglwysfach.[7] In retrospect, RS recognizes that the bullishness of these parishioners exposed his personal vulnerabilities, lurking deficiencies which had been unaddressed in Manafon, what he calls his 'weak hold' on his identity.[8] If the culture of the Eglwysfach is hostile, the great Welsh university at Aberystwyth also disappoints: it is not the source of intellectual inspiration that he expected.

Fleeing from the expectations of these domineering parishioners, what does draw and delight RS is the natural world which surrounds Eglwysfach. In the birds, mountains, woods and moorlands he finds freedom for the spirit which the church inhibits. A poem from this period, 'The Moor', confides how the troubled vicar becomes a refugee walking in the wilderness of Wales, escaping the personal diminishments and spiritual frustrations of parish life.

> It was like a church to me.
> I entered it on soft foot,
> Breath held like a cap in the hand.
> It was quiet.
> What God was there made himself felt,
> Not listened to, in clean colours
> That brought a moistening of the eye,
> In movement of the wind over grass.
>
> There were no prayers said. But stillness
> Of the heart's passions – that was praise

Enough; and the mind's cessation
Of its kingdom. I walked on,
Simple and poor, while the air crumbled
And broke on me generously as bread.[9]

For RS, it is in solitary encounter that true religious experience is to be found, rather than in the suffocating wrangles of church life.

Vicar of Aberdaron (1967–78) and retirement in Llŷn: the priest as Astronaut

'He had reached the destination of his own personal pilgrimage' RS writes of his arrival in Aberdaron.[10] In this parish on the western-most tip of the beautiful Llŷn peninsula, with its coastal church looking out to Bardsey, the holy island of ancient pilgrimage, and its rich and lively heritage of Welsh culture, RS had found the perfect place in which to write and to minister. It seemed like entering into a kind of spiritual and artistic homeland, and here some of R. S. Thomas's most compelling poetry is written. Poems such as 'The Kingdom', 'The Bright Field' and 'Sea Watching' speak of his glimpses of God's seemingly fleeting presence with profound eloquence and simplicity. But there is conflict here too. The ministerial expertise accrued over many years of faithful service does not simplify the task of pastoring, taking the priest deeper into a complicated and disturbing involvement with the complex mystery of human pain and sinfulness. The praying poet who contemplates the mystery of God with profound attentiveness finds that language fails him as he encounters the vastness of God's silence, hiddenness and unpredictable beauty. Though he has reached a certain degree of public recognition as a poet, he is a severe critic of his own work. Writing on the eve of his seventieth birthday he says:

There is certainly no feeling of achievement at all, but rather a falling short of what I would have wished to achieve. The sort of yardsticks I have chosen ... when one falls short of those one knows one hasn't been chosen.[11]

RS feels more strongly than ever that his art and his faith are insignificant in the present culture. He finds himself attending to the creative tension within himself as a priest, a person of prayer and as a poet – the clash between the spiritual perception arising from the religious perspective of the poetic imagination, versus the rational scientific hegemony of Western materialism, with its worship of the market, its negation of the past and its ruination of the natural environment. He finds Llŷn overrun with English tourists and constantly disturbed by screaming RAF jets practising war manoeuvres. Yet, if poetry is to have any voice in a techno-logical age it must come to understand and use the language of science within its own art, just as theology must adapt to speak to a critical, scientific age – the challenges of a new era gnaw at the poet and the priest in his final years.

In *Neb*, R. S. Thomas is candid about the practical challenges of retirement from full-time stipendiary ministry. He does not want to leave Aberdaron vicarage, which is spacious enough for all his books, familiar furniture and Elsie's paintings. Their retirement home nearby, though beautifully located, is tiny and inconvenient. He faces the challenges of negotiating appropriate responsibility for his ageing mother who lives some distance away, and of caring for his wife who has a deteriorating illness which affects her eyesight. He asks the bishop to be allowed to stay on a house-for-duty basis, but his request is refused. So the final transition from full-time ministry into retirement does not bring with it a sense of completion, or relief, or even loss. It is an ambiguous time, for while it gives him what every artistic spirit needs to be productive – 'the main prerequisites of the creative mind, time and silence'[12] – this period is also full of unexpected difficulty and a profound sense of alienation. So in the relative freedom and leisure of retirement R. S. Thomas finds himself setting out on strange and uncharted journeys within. Developing the journey metaphor of Coleridge's ballad 'The Ancient Mariner', RS's poem 'The New Mariner' describes his experience of spiritual odyssey in the language of space travel. Even in this period of professional accomplishment and personal maturity, the priest-poet is dismayed by God's elusiveness:

... I had looked forward
to old age as a time
of quietness, a time to draw
my horizons about me,
to watch memories ripening
in the sunlight of a walled garden.
But there is the void
over my head and the distance
within that the tireless signals
come from. And astronaut
on impossible journeys
to the far side of the self
I return with messages
I cannot decipher, garrulous
about them, worrying the ear
of the passer-by, hot on his way
to the marriage of plain fact with plain fact.[13]

Just as in Jesus's parable of God's kingdom (Luke 14.15–24), those invited are too busy with priorities of their own to come to the feast of wisdom set for them by poetry and faith. So the priest-poet feels himself to be on the cultural margins, his message about God unheeded by busy people rushing on to meet the next important target. The poet-priest finds himself having become a nuisance, a bothersome distraction, trying to speak through poetry and religion of an alternative reality to busy people who are deaf to his language. Retirement proves to be a time of disturbance for the priest, both in his spiritual life and in his outlook on contemporary culture and its values. Yet this very dissatisfaction impels RS into public campaigning and community organizing – the formation of a branch of Welsh CND and fundraising for the purchase of Bardsey as a nature reserve to protect the natural environment from the degradation of commercial exploitation by unsympathetic farming methods and crass tourism. The pastoral discomfort between priest and people which the metaphors of fugitive and astronaut suggest is the stimulus for creative action and innovation. At the same time solitary the metaphors speak of a spiritual resilience in the priest and a costly commitment to pursuing the spiritual life in the context of pastoral ministry. However uncomfortable and subversive of pastoral idealism, RS resists evading what is painful and difficult in his poetic reflections on the experience of ministry.

Conclusion

R. S. Thomas's poems and autobiography give us a sense of personal pilgrimage in which the journey is a continual seeking-out of 'the right place' to minister as a priest and be creative as a poet: the pursuit of an environment in which he might flourish and enable others to flourish. For Thomas, factors that might make a context fruitful are particular: proximity to mountains, moorland and sea which allows his mind, body and soul to roam free; and a community in which the Welsh language is spoken by the majority, where Welsh culture and history shape communal life and foster the contemporary imagination. But at each successive stage of this journey there is the experience of tension within himself between 'ideal' personal need and 'actual' dimensions of the place, a sense of personal dissatisfaction which is both unsettling and challenging, yet also generative, so that the priest-poet is *in* but not *of* the place and its people – a difference which fires him to be prophetic as a pastor and eloquent as a poet. This yearning for the right place impels him in a deepening search for the source and wellspring of his poetic, priestly art – 'the stuff his roots were made of'[14] – an artistic-spiritual pilgrimage which is lifelong and unresolved.

R. S. Thomas's reflective approach to ministry enables him to trace this journey and to construct a sense of meaning out of his experiences. The meanings shift and change, they deepen, swirl, thicken and evaporate like the tide, and the mode in which he reflects – through autobiography and poetry – enables him to capture and contain, or to hold for only a moment, the complex, contradictory, fleeting and recurring material of the self-in-relation to God and to the mystery of God disclosed or hidden in others, in creation, and most wonderfully in the mystery of self.

The long-term practice of reflection in R. S. Thomas's ministry is a discipline for clergy to consider. The substance of his reflection is significant too: the inter-relationship between priestly and personal identity is the territory in which the creativity of the artist and the minister flourishes or falters, and the mode of RS's reflection – through poems and the autobiographical journal – allows him to be an explorer in the landscape of himself. Ministerial reflection needs literary, artistic, expressive modes like this which allow the heart to speak and the person to emerge in all the occasional untidiness of our motivations and the sometimes confused and painful sense of purpose which may be both mystifying as well as profoundly mysterious.

Acknowledgements

The author gratefully acknowledges permission to quote from the poems of R. S. Thomas, copyright © Kunjana Thomas, first published in the following collections:

'Pilgrimages' from *Frequencies*, London: Macmillan, 1978, p. 51.
'They Keep Me Sober' from *The Echoes Return Slow*, London: Macmillan, 1988, p. 63.
'A Priest to His People' from *The Stones of the Field*, The Druid Press, 1946.
'I Was Vicar of Large Things' from *The Echoes Return Slow*, p. 25.
'The Moor' from *Pietà*, London: Rupert Hart-Davis, 1966, p. 24.
'The New Mariner' from *Between Here and Now*, London: Macmillan, 1981, p. 99.

Notes

1. R. S. Thomas, *Neb*, in J. Walford Davies, *Autobiographies*, translated 1997, London: J. M. Dent, 1985.
2. From 'Pilgrimages', *Frequencies*, London: Macmillan, 1978, p. 51.
3. 'They Keep Me Sober' from *The Echoes Return Slow*, London: Macmillan, 1988, p. 63.

4. 'A Priest to His People' from *The Stones of the Field*, The Druid Press, 1946.

5. 'I Was Vicar of Large Things' from *The Echoes Return Slow*, p. 5.

6. Justin Wintle, *Furious Interiors: Wales, R. S. Thomas and God*, London: HarperCollins, 1996, p. 163.

7. *The Echoes Return Slow*, p. 46.

8. *Neb*, p. 74.

9. 'The Moor' from *Pietà*, London: Rupert Hart-Davis, 1966, p. 24.

10. *Neb*, p. 77.

11. Letter to Raymond Garlick, 27 March 1983, in Byron Rogers, *The Man Who Went Into the West: The Life of R. S. Thomas*, London: Aurum Press, 2006, p. 279.

12. *Neb*, p. 91.

13. 'The New Mariner' from *Between Here and Now*, London: Macmillan, 1981, p. 99.

14. *Neb*, p. 56.

7

Body Building and Moving On with Liturgy

MARK BEACH

As a newly appointed incumbent I was invited to tea with one of my predecessors. His wife had got the silver teapot out and there were neat sandwiches awaiting my arrival. We had a very pleasant afternoon and, as I was about to leave, the elderly clergyman said, 'Mark, I have just one piece of advice for you. Rector means ruler, never forget that.' I have never forgotten it, but probably not for the reasons he intended. This chapter starts by reflecting on my theological understanding of the place of the minister in the life of the Church – the things I am learning and have never forgotten. It continues by exploring the implications for such an understanding on our liturgical practice, and concludes with a brief reflection on leaving the parish.

Leadership

My theological understanding of the place of a minister within the life of the Church is based on this somewhat prosaic but nonetheless inspiring passage by Robin Greenwood:

The quality of the relation between priest and people may be expressed as an unwritten mandate. The priest, in a spirit of vulnerability, is saying: 'Although I believe I have been called simultaneously by you, the bishop and God, to be your parish priest, please never forget that I am also, like you, a baptised member of this congregation.' On their part, it is as though the people were saying, in a spirit of openness: 'Yes, we are glad to hear you acknowledge that at heart you are one of us by baptism, but we ask you, for as long as it seems right from both sides, to be president of this local community in a spirit of persuasive and courteous leadership.'[1]

From Greenwood's *Transforming Priesthood*, this passage has been something of a mantra for me since I first read it; so much so that when I began work in Rugby it formed a part of the institution liturgy. It sets out what I believe underlies the relationship that is key to the success of collaborative working in the life of the Church. It is a mutuality based on the common baptism of each member of the Body of Christ which also recognizes that the ordained person is called to exercise 'persuasive and courteous' leadership within the community.

However, Greenwood leaves unanswered the nature of the relationship between the baptized and those who are additionally ordained. This question is addressed by Stephen Pickard, an Australian bishop, whose *Theological Foundations for Collaborative Ministry* provided another 'wow' moment in the development of my own thinking. Pickard speaks of 'dynamically ordered relationships'.[2] He describes this in a lengthy quotation, which bears repeating here:

> Ministries at all levels are co-related, integrally and dynamically linked and in this way establish each other. They exhibit a genuine complementarity between an emergent ministerial order and a 'top-down' influence. Thus those higher level ministries act in such a way that the energy of the various ministries is released and directed for the purposes of the whole ecclesial system. The higher order ministries are thus confirmed in their purpose and significance as the 'lower ordered' ministries fulfil themselves in accord with the purposes of the whole. In this way the orders of ministry establish each other and foster each other's work and purpose. Thus it can be truly said that the ministry of the higher orders and the orders that brought them forth bring each other into being.[3]

Pickard's 'genuine complementarity' is based not on goodwill, as is often the case in practice and which runs the risk of a failure of that goodwill wreaking havoc or a change of personalities bringing it to an end. Instead Pickard emphasizes that both the baptized and the ordained are dependent on each other for the well-being of the whole Church.

Often this is in spite of rather than because of the understanding of leadership that is held by clergy, which is all too often a top-down model with paternalistic overtones, even among female clergy and modelling an heroic or messianic style. Anecdotal evidence of this is to be found in the often overheard remark of curates saying 'When I get my own parish …'. Michael Sadgrove in his *Wisdom and Ministry* proposes that leadership should be formed through the 'heart work' of parochial life and 'calls for real wisdom'.[4] Thus instead of an heroic model of leadership, I suggest we should search for a post-heroic model which is wise, gentle and persuasive, combining the insights of Greenwood, Pickard and Sadgrove. Here there will be no place for the ordained person lording it over the parish, no place for top-down leadership, and the language of interregna will be banned for ever!

Leadership in this model will be based on the learned experience of parochial life, much like Stanley Hauerwas's virtue ethics in which the role of the teacher is to model the way of living and of the community to live it day by day. Thus my wise, gentle and persuasive leadership is to be formed and lived out in the whole Church, not just in its ordained leadership.

Being the Body of Christ

This model of leadership is thoroughly biblical. Taking Paul's image of the Body of Christ (1 Cor. 12.12–31) we can see that there is no place for hierarchical, top-down leadership in the life of the Body, rather each part is dependent on the rest for its well-being. Of course, there is a place for leadership, for risk taking and for encouraging the people of God to follow where the Spirit is leading, but only in a manner that is based around wise, gentle and persuasive leadership. In many places, and in many aspects of the life of the Church, the relationship is lived out effectively and informs the practice of contemporary ministry, ministry which is shared in ways that could not have been imagined 20 years ago; and not just in those areas that the clergy choose to delegate!

In all of this I am reminded of a sermon by St Augustine:

> So if you want to understand the body of Christ, listen to the apostle telling the faithful, You, though, are the body of Christ and its members (1 Cor. 12.27). So if it's you that are the body of Christ and its members, it's the mystery meaning you that has been placed on the Lord's table; what you receive is the mystery that means you. It is to what you are that you reply Amen, and by so replying you express your assent. What you hear, you see, is The body of Christ, and you answer, Amen. So be a member of the body of Christ, in order to make that Amen true.

And later:

> Ponder and rejoice! Unity, truth, piety, charity – one bread! And what is this one bread? 'We who are many are one body!' Remember that bread is not made from a single grain of wheat, but from many. When you were exorcised, it was like a grinding. When you were baptized, it was like being mixed into dough. When you received the fire of the Holy Spirit, it was like being baked. So be what you can see, and become what you are. (Augustine, Sermon 272)

C. W. McPherson, writing in *Cross Currents*, expresses the centrality of this idea to pastoral ministry:

> I cannot avoid Augustine now, as a parish priest, since his simple injunction to 'become what you are' so powerfully and paradoxically expresses our relationship to our baptismal vows.[5]

In my liturgical practice I have adapted these words into a form for administering Holy Communion: 'Become what you are, the Body of Christ'. Here we have a striking paradox. It is paradoxical because it invites the baptized member of the Church to become something that she already is: a part of the Body of Christ. The point of the paradox, however, is that she should become more fully what she already is, by participating in a meal during which the body of Christ is offered, shared and received. I have summed this paradox up by saying: 'We come together as the Body of Christ, to receive the Body of Christ in order to become the Body of Christ.'

Second, the paradox is challenging because it requires the communicant to move away from an individualistic approach to Holy Communion, often expressed in the approach to the altar rail as 'my walk to God' or as 'making my communion' into a view of receiving Communion as a corporate act in which the whole community becomes the active participants in the mission of Christ to the world. My 'words at the giving of Communion' can therefore be interpreted as addressed serially to each communicant and yet they contain an invitation to be more fully a part of something much larger than one individual, the Body of Christ; not a private relationship but a public one shared with all others at the same rail and, more widely, with communicants around the world. In this sense Holy Communion becomes a political act, one that builds up the *politeia*, the Body of Christ.

Here, there is a parallel with my suggested move away from 'when I get my parish ...' into a more communal expression of both the life of the communicant and the ordained person exercising wise leadership. The practice, of offering Holy Communion in this way, brought to mind what I found to be a startling revelation. There is one glaring area in which these principles of participation in the Body and its leadership as lived out by the baptized and the ordained are not embedded into the life of the Church, and that is in her liturgy; and yet I suggest this is the very place in which the relationship should be most clearly expressed and lived out.

The shape of the Body

I say this in response to the claim by Sam Wells, in his *God's Companions: Reimagining Christian Ethics*, that God gives to his people abundantly all that they need in order to become his 'companions'.[6] By 'God's companion', he literally means the one who shares bread with God. This sharing of bread is precisely that action which forms the Body of Christ. Wells uses Dom Gregory Dix's seminal work on the Eucharist, *The Shape of the Liturgy* which provides a framework around which Eucharistic worship is seen to be built. Dix suggests that there is a 'standard structure' to the Eucharist which, with an 'intricate pattern of local variety' is universally apparent, having its beginnings in the Jewish roots of Christian worship but surviving to this day.[7]

This notion of the 'shape of the liturgy' has influenced the work of Stanley Hauerwas and Samuel Wells. Together they have edited the *Blackwell's Companion to Christian Ethics*, in which they deliberately use the Eucharistic shape as an outline for their work. Hauerwas offers a justification of this approach to the teaching of Christian Ethics in his *In Good Company*. In particular, the essay 'The Liturgical Shape of Christian Life: Teaching Christian Ethics as Worship' explains that the approach is based on the 'presumption that there is literally nothing more important for the Christian people to do than to praise God' and that the goal of the approach is to make clear that 'Christians are not simply called to do the "right thing" but rather are expected to be holy.'[8] This holiness is not based on a personal devotion, reading of scripture or the regular reception of Holy Communion, but in Hauerwas's view, on the participation within the community as it engages the worship of God. Thus we can see emerging in Hauerwas's work both the transformative effect of Christian worship, which develops in the individual the virtue of holiness, and also the uniqueness of the *politeia* that is created through worship and especially 'Eucharistic communion'.

Hauerwas uses the various sections of the 'shape of the liturgy' to illustrate what he says about the various ethical topics he covers. So for example his consideration of race, class and gender takes place in relation to confession and sin while he links the offering of the Eucharist with economic justice, war and peace. This emphasis on worship and its central role in the formation of both the individual and the whole Christian community is further developed by Samuel Wells in an article in *Studies in*

Christian Ethics entitled 'How Common Worship forms Local Character'.[9] His argument here is amplified considerably in *God's Companions: Reimagining Christian Ethics*[10] although many of the examples he gives are the same in both works. Wells's premise that God gives to his people abundantly all that they need in order to become his 'companions' may be challenged in the light of our liturgical practice. By 'God's companion', he literally means the one who shares bread with God. He then lists a series of occasions in St Luke's Gospel in which Jesus shares food with his friends through which the gift of companionship is established.[11] This gift is 'habit forming'[12] inasmuch as it provides, in Hauerwas's terms, not only the means by which a Christian will discover how to do the right thing but it is also the pathway to holiness. In this way the individual is transformed by his encounter with God and, as a communal act, the unique *politeia* is established.

Liturgical pinch points

In this light I am now going to look briefly at four areas of the liturgy, or actions, in which Wells sees this 'habit forming gift' in operation and the examples that he gives to illustrate these areas.

Gathering

First, the Gathering or Meeting. Wells likens this to the warming up of an orchestra on stage prior to a concert: individual instruments can be heard tuning and practising difficult passages, but their purpose is the performance of the symphony. So the participants in worship gather, amidst preparations and catch-up conversation; but this group of individuals also gathers with a purpose, to become the Body of Christ. I have described this as the *politeia*, but Wells describes it as the 'Congregation (*grex* = crowd + *con* = together)'.[13] This congregation is very diverse and comes from all sorts of different places with different expectations but: 'It takes all these kinds of people to make a Eucharist.'[14] But the gathering is more than just a coming together of a diverse group of people; essentially it is coming together to eat a shared meal and, to use Wells's image, just as a newly married couple discover things about each other through sharing meals, so the Church discovers about its nature as a congregation or *politeia* through this shared meal. The example that Wells offers of the Gathering is a congregation in which the presiding minister asks the congregation about how each person expects to meet with God in worship that day. 'In doing so, they heightened one another's awareness of the wealth of understanding and experience gathered in that place of meeting on that day.'[15] In another place the furniture was rearranged so that instead of looking at the back of each other's heads, they looked at each other and saw instead of the rather plain building in which they worshipped, the beauty of each other, expressing something of the congregation that has been formed.

A good starting point for the expression of the 'dynamically ordered relationship' is in the simple greeting that often opens liturgical worship, called in *Common Worship* The Gathering. However, this is the first of my liturgical pinch points. The text and enacting of the *Common Worship* Gathering are in my opinion a very significant weakness, and yet it is relatively easy to solve. The people gather in worship, coming from their diverse backgrounds with different priorities, they often even come in by different doors. The opening words of our liturgy form that diverse gathering of individuals into the Body of Christ as described by Greenwood. But the words lack a sense of mutuality and instead communicate just the kind of hierarchical model of the Church that more properly belongs to an earlier age.

The Lord be with you.
All: And also with you.

These words are designed to 'gather' the community as the Body of Christ for the transforming act of worship. The exchange sums up the dynamic relationship between priest and people. Without either voice neither forms the Body of Christ in worship and yet it remains a bald exchange, which although constituting the Body does nothing to describe the transformative nature of that encounter. Even the rubric which states that 'the people and priest greet

each other in the Lord's name'[16] pays scant acknowledgement to
the diversity of those who gather, nor to the creation of the congregation. By comparison, the Sunday Morning Communion of
the Iona Community[17] has the following Opening Response:

Leader	Welcome to this ancient place.
All	**House of prayer for many nations, home to all who come.**
Leader	Welcome to this gathering place.
All	**Friend and stranger, saint and sinner in all who gather here.**
Leader	Come with hope or hesitation; come with joy or yearning; all who hunger, all who thirst for life in all its fullness.
All	**Generous God and Generous saviour, touch us through your spirit.**

Here we can see that the power of texts used in worship have
to radically re-represent the relationship within the Church and
especially between ordained and non-ordained such that our
liturgy embodies the 'dynamically ordered relationship' advocated
by Pickard. Wells's liturgical actions powerfully form the Body but
do they not also need powerful words to describe what is going on?

Being reconciled

The second action is that of 'being reconciled'. Wells says that
this consists of four aspects although, for reasons of space, I shall
focus only on the confession aspect.[18] This is another area in
which both the individual and corporate aspects of Christian worship are revealed, as Wells says: 'From personal repentance the
congregation begin to articulate corporate confession.'[19] In one of
the examples that Wells gives from a local congregation he speaks
of the practice of two people coming forward from the congregation to confess by forming a human sculpture:

> ... kneeling upright. Facing one another, heads resting on each
> other's shoulders ... the statue proclaimed that there is no rec-

onciliation with God without reconciliation with neighbour, and that each neighbour is as broken and needy as the other.[20]

Once again the experience of worshipping together has formed the gathering into a unique congregation.

But the confession is another example of the weakness of *Common Worship*[21] texts to adequately express the relationship between the baptized and the ordained:

> Almighty God, our heavenly Father,
> we have sinned against you
> and against our neighbour
> in thought and word and deed,
> through negligence, through weakness,
> through our own deliberate fault.
> We are truly sorry
> and repent of all our sins.
> For the sake of your Son Jesus Christ,
> who died for us,
> forgive us all that is past
> and grant that we may serve you in newness of life
> to the glory of your name.
> **Amen.**

While the language is plural the emphasis is on the individual and it lacks an emphasis on relationships within the Body of Christ. The following alternative text comes closer with its emphasis on the neighbour, but again makes no reference to the gathering of the assembly and each person's responsibility to the other:

> Most merciful God,
> Father of our Lord Jesus Christ,
> we confess that we have sinned
> in thought, word and deed.
> We have not loved you with our whole heart.
> We have not loved our neighbours as ourselves.
> In your mercy
> forgive what we have been,

help us to amend what we are,
and direct what we shall be;
that we may do justly,
love mercy,
and walk humbly with you, our God.
Amen.

Even the more responsorial penitential texts in *Common Worship* lack this emphasis and so we have to look once again to the Iona Community for a text with a far stronger corporate emphasis.[22]

Leader	Before God, with the people of God, I confess to my brokenness; to the ways I wound my life, the lives of others and the life of the world.
All	**May God forgive you, Christ renew you, and the Spirit enable you to grow in love.**
Leader	Amen.
All	**Before God, with the people of God, we confess to our brokenness; to the ways we wound our lives, the lives of others and the life of the world.**
Leader	May God forgive you, Christ renew you, and the Spirit enable you to grow in love.
All	**Amen.**

Not only are confession and absolution combined, suggesting a great sense of corporate-ness within the congregation, but also the use of the plural pronoun in the congregational text implies the move from individual to corporate that Wells envisages, but which does not occur in the texts, and a sense of belonging to one another.

The Peace

The third area I want to mention is that of the Peace, which again concerns the issues of reconciliation. But here we see the 'deepest resonances' as the reconciliation proclaimed follows both reconciliation in absolution, the hearing of the word, the response by means of an Affirmation of Faith and an expression of compassion though Intercession.[23] And at this point in worship a new concept is raised, as Wells puts it:

> It is not just that in the broken Body of Christ the Church finds peace with God. It is not just that the Eucharist makes the Church one Body. It is that the Church cannot eat one body unless it is one body. Otherwise, it eats and drinks judgment on itself (1 Corinthians 11.29).[24]

Once again, the paradoxical nature of what the congregation (or *politeia*) is and has the potential to become emerges to challenge the Church, and as Wells says, 'This creates a significant urgency' through which the Church has to decide whether or not to continue with the Eucharist ensuring that it does not 'eat and drink judgment on itself'.

However, once again I believe that the texts let us down, they are bland and do not, at this crucial moment in the liturgy, convey anything more than a gentle, verbal nod towards the reality of the Body gathered for worship.

The default text goes like this:

The president may introduce the Peace with a suitable sentence, and then says
We are the Body of Christ, by the one spirit we were all baptized into one body, let us then pursue all that makes for peace and builds up our common life.
The peace of the Lord be always with you
All: and also with you.
These words may be added
Let us offer one another a sign of peace.
All may exchange a sign of peace.

I recognize that exchanging the Peace is not a universally loved part of contemporary liturgy; however, surely some stronger expression of the nature of the Body can be created without causing discomfort to those who would rather live in a peace-free zone!

The sharing of food

The final area I want to consider is that of the sharing of food. Here we come to the climax of eucharistic worship, it is here that each of the constituent parts, including those I have not discussed, find their completion 'so that the members of the congregation may become the body of Christ, and he might live in and through the Church'.[25] Wells describes this sharing of food by returning to the theme of the abundance of God's provision that it enacts. This abundance is seen in the 'discovery that the more food is shared, the more food there is',[26] in recognizing that there are a limitless number of places around the table and in learning to be aware of the diversity of the people gathered around the table. The awareness that the Eucharist proclaims the abundance, even 'superabundance' is in itself a political statement calling the Church to a distinctive pattern of life. It is a:

> virtuous circle of never ending provision – this is the embodiment of God's call to his people to worship him (the offering), to be his friends (the sharing), and to eat with him (the receiving). It is not so much that God desires Christians to match his sacrifice with their sacrifice; it is more that he moves Christians to respond to his fulsome pouring-out with their own kenotic imitation.[27]

The examples that Wells offers of the sharing of food include a discussion about posture. A congregation debated for some time about the posture they should adopt to receive Communion. Standing, kneeling and sitting were all debated. In the end they decided to stand in a circle around the altar which 'stressed the differences of height, age and physical disability and made it necessary for some to rest on the strength of others'. But this was not a universally acceptable decision:

> some said they felt unworthy to stand, others pointed out that Christ has enabled, even commanded them to stand and that their standing was a symbol of the resurrection. By standing in a circle, the congregation realised they did not just eat of one body – they were one body.[28]

However, I suspect that this is a somewhat idealistic view, both in terms of how the liturgy is enacted in many places and, perhaps more significantly, in the texts that are provided in *Common Worship*, which seldom enable the worshipper to be transformed by his encounter with God and formed, more fully, into the Body of Christ.

There are again texts that give a stronger sense of coming together as the Body of Christ, for example the worship song written by Ian Wilson:

> Come to the table of the Lord.
> Not because you must but because you may.
> Not to show you're righteous but to follow in His way.
> Come to the table of the Lord.

There are also liturgical texts of other traditions, for example the Iona Community, that more fully realize this potential.[29]

> Come to this table,
> you who have much faith
> and you who would like to have more;
> you who have been here often
> and you who have not been here for a long time;
> you who have tried to follow Jesus
> and you who have failed. Come.
> It is Christ who invites us to meet him here.

Leaving the parish

I hope that I have shown that by relatively simple changes to our liturgical texts and practices we can embody our theology of ministry in our worship more completely. I believe that, and so when I recently left the parish I had served for nine years we worked on some liturgy to help us to reveal meaning in the departure. Here is a simple text, which we adapted for the purpose and which enabled both the congregation and I to express how we were feeling.

The Congregation speaks to Mark:
As you journey onward,
We give thanks for all that you have given us,
We ask forgiveness where we have failed you,
And we ask God's blessing on our continuing journey.

A moment of silence

Mark speaks to the assembled company:
As I journey onward,
I give thanks for all that you have given me,
I ask forgiveness where I have failed you,
And I ask God's blessing on my continuing journey.[30]

After this, the churchwardens received the church keys, removed the rector's cope from my shoulders and I walked from the church. I felt the power of the occasion and it helped the process of parting and I believe that others were helped too.

There are those who argue that worship should not be the place for scoring theological points, and yet if our worship fails to adequately describe the nature of the worshipping community, then, I suggest, it is failing in its role to build up the Body of Christ.

Notes

1. Robin Greenwood, *Transforming Priesthood: A New Theology of Mission and Ministry*, London: SPCK, 1994, p. 157.

2. Stephen Pickard, *Theological Foundations for Collaborative Ministry*, Farnham: Ashgate, 2009, p. 141.

3. Pickard, *Theological Foundations*, p. 142.

4. Michael Sadgrove, *Wisdom and Ministry: The Call to Leadership*, London: SPCK, 2008, pp. 8f.

5. C. W. McPherson, 'Augustine Our Contemporary', *Cross Currents*, 50, Spring–Summer 2000.

6. Sam Wells, *God's Companions: Reimagining Christian Ethics*, Oxford: Wiley-Blackwell, 2006, p. 18.

7. Gregory Dix, *The Shape of the Liturgy*, London: A. & C. Black, 1945, p. xiii.

8. Stanley Hauerwas, 'The Liturgical Shape of Christian Life', in *In Good Company*, Indiana: University of Notre Dame Press, 1995, pp. 154ff.

9. Sam Wells, 'How *Common Worship* forms Local Character', *Studies in Christian Ethics*, 15(1), 2002.

10. See Note 6 above.

11. Wells, *God's Companions*, p. 27.

12. Wells, *God's Companions*, p. 12.

13. Wells, *God's Companions*, p. 127.

14. Wells, *God's Companions*, p. 128.

15. Wells, *God's Companions*, p. 132.

16. *Common Worship: Services and Prayers for the Church of England*, London: Church House Publishing, 2000, p. 166.

17. *Iona Abbey Worship Book*, Glasgow: Wild Goose Publications, 2001, p. 3.

18. Wells, *God's Companions*, p. 143.

19. Wells, *God's Companions*, p. 145.

20. Wells, *God's Companions*, p. 147.

21. I recognize that this strays into the area of authorized texts. I offer this example not as an inducement to law breaking but as an encouragement to reflect on how we can develop our liturgical practice and language in the light of contemporary thinking on the nature of the Church.

22. *Iona Abbey Worship Book*, p. 16.

23. Wells, *God's Companions*, p. 186.

24. Wells, *God's Companions*, p. 186.

25. Wells, *God's Companions*, p. 211.

26. Wells, *God's Companions*, p. 211.

27. Wells, *God's Companions*, p. 212.

28. Wells, *God's Companions*, pp. 212ff.

29. *Iona Abbey Worship Book* (see note 17 above).

30. Adapted from *Daily Office SSF: Human Rites*, revised edn, London: Mowbray, 2010.

8

From Parish to Chaplaincy

ANTHONY BUCKLEY

Henrietta is vicar of a growing parish church and believes she might be called to school chaplaincy. She considers applying to a school. There is much about the job description that excites her, especially the privilege of representing and expressing the Church, the love of God in action, with so many people every day. She is to be responsible for spiritual and pastoral welfare; it is expected that she will build relationships with staff and parents as well as pupils, and so the wider school community she serves will be about 4,000 people. There she will be, a priest of the Church of England, in the midst of them all.

But she is disturbed when she is told by her bishop that 'it is a shame you are thinking of leaving mainstream ministry'. The conversation unsettles her. Is there an implication that her ministry in a school will matter less to the Church than her ministry in a parish? It seems strange that pastoral, liturgical and evangelistic ministry to a community of this size is not seen as 'mainstream'. She picks up a book on chaplaincy, and is not encouraged by these words: 'Many chaplains report that once they take a chaplaincy job they find they are perceived to have marginalized themselves, placing themselves outside the boundaries of the church.'[1]

Henrietta also begins to wonder if it will be difficult to return to parish ministry, or to seek a position of wider responsibility in the Church. She continues to read her book. 'Time spent working in chaplaincies is sometimes considered to be irrelevant experience when a priest is looking for a parish or diocesan post. Yet a chaplain may have gained considerable experience of managing a team and/or a budget, and has probably received a great deal more management training than a priest who has spent his or her career entirely in parish ministry.'[2] Might future doors be closed to Henrietta if she has a season in chaplaincy? Is she burning her boats?

But there is also much encouragement. The constant contact with people sounds as if it will be energizing and relevant; and there are some in the Church, particularly those with a heart for mission, who are supportive of her move.

This chapter will explore what Henrietta, and those like her, might be learning in this experience. The focus will largely be on school chaplaincy, but it is hoped that some of the points will have wider relevance. Henrietta senses God's call, she thinks she will learn a great deal, she is seeking to be Christ to her neighbour and she longs for growth in the kingdom. But some parts of the Church feel she has sold out, and make it clear that she is no longer truly 'one of us'. How will she cope with her change in role, with these contrasting views about what she is doing providing an uncertain backdrop?

* * *

Transition always involves loss and there cannot be change without it. It is helpful to be honest about what has been left behind. This is true of a move from parish to parish, but the changes can be all the more pronounced between parish and chaplaincy.

A chaplain may have given up:

Being a vicar

Henrietta has lost the privilege of shepherding the gathered people of God from the parish on those occasions she enjoyed so much. Chapel services at school (if the school has a chapel) carry a similar privilege, but she is less likely to have three generations of the same family present at the same time. She might miss the quiet magic of Midnight Communion or the joyfully chaotic harvest service, or simply the sense of deep satisfaction at the end of a good Sunday. The faithful people in the services had wanted to be there; she is now faced with the challenge of leading services or assemblies where often the congregation is compelled to be there. She has left behind the vicarage and the status, the roles and an important place in liturgical processions (which she was beginning rather to enjoy).

She has also left behind the leaking roof, the worries about the parish share and the difficulty of living in a large vicarage without much money. She has left behind the difficult church member.

Having an unusually high level of job and accommodation security

In his first term as a school chaplain Henry realizes that he does not see eye to eye with the senior management about the way he is leading assemblies and that word is spreading that his classroom control is not always sound. The headmaster calls him in and reminds him that he is on probation for the first year. He remembers that as a vicar his job and housing were secure. They are not now. To his shame he recalls that when he was in parish ministry he was rather skilled at blaming failure on other circumstances, or would simply drop one project and start another (which his PCC found slightly tiring, but did not tell him). In his school he has to improve what he is doing or he will be out.

Susan remembered that the vicarage did have its drawbacks, but she knew there was a helpful and efficient diocesan support system in place. As a hospital chaplain in the north of the country she has been able to buy a flat. This excites her, but she is quickly reminded that looking after a property brings its own costs and responsibilities.

Having authority

An archdeacon said to Sam, 'How are you going to feel about not being in charge?' Sam felt he was a collaborative parish priest. He always ticked the 'committed to working in a team' box on leadership courses. About to be an army chaplain he now realizes that when he was a vicar he exercised considerable power.

Yes, there was a team, but a nod or word from him was what really mattered. As a chaplain he is not the central figure. He is no longer running the show. (Perhaps he should not have been 'running the show' in the parish, but that is outside the scope of this chapter.)

Sam offers to help at a local church when his army duties allow. The vicar is grateful and includes Sam on the rota, but there are no staff meetings and he never has time to discuss anything with him. Sam feels a bit out of things.

Being in the loop

As does Samantha, working as a university chaplain. But for her it is the deanery and diocese that seem to be circles from which she is excluded. She does not receive all the communications that her parish colleagues do. She has to ask three times to get a diocesan directory. Deanery chapter meetings are held during normal working hours; it is very difficult to attend.

Being understood

James became a school chaplain. He heard that one senior official in the Church of England said about him that 'he just wasn't willing to get his hands dirty'. A bishop said about Philip, another chaplain, 'He has been lured away.' These were uncharitable accusations, and were hurtful to the individuals concerned. Both had prayerfully sought to discern God's calling and now here were senior colleagues making disparaging comments behind their backs and misunderstanding their motives.

Being on sure liturgical ground

It is customary for Cynthia to invite the local incumbent to take part in a special service of remembrance for stillborn children in her hospital chapel. But she has heard that the new vicar has rigid views on liturgy; she knows many of these mums and dads and feels it is not the time to be pedantic about such words. Who will be setting the agenda for the service?

Being in an explicitly spiritual ethos

Rupert had enjoyed being curate in a thriving and happy church. He loved the shared values and purpose. In his school the ethos is not quite the same. Sometimes he does not agree with the way the school is going – is there a culture of manipulating course choices to get better results to hit targets that no one believes in? As a curate, at least half the people he regularly met shared his faith (he would have liked to have met more people from outside the church family, but time often disappeared). As a chaplain, it is less than a tenth. Exciting for mission, but it can feel spiritually isolating.

The family having a place of honour

There is a privilege in a church about being the children of the vicar. Church members are likely to be friendly and chocolate eggs arrive at Easter. Children of a chaplain have no such status. They have to find their own way into church life, like any other young person. This may bring the attraction of anonymity, but it can bring a sense of bereavement.

But ... on the bright side

Chaplains may sometimes feel on the fringes of parish, deanery, diocesan life, but there is much to be thankful for. A chaplain is part of a ready-made community that is usually supportive and appreciative, whereas it can be lonely being in charge of a parish. Depending on the nature of the chaplaincy, there can be a great deal of immediate and positive feedback, which does not always happen in parish life. There can be the joy of seeing voluntary congregations in the workplace growing (compulsory chapel brings a different challenge). The chaplain is unlikely to have the practical and administrative concerns of looking after a parish church and a team of volunteers. He or she does not have the pressure and worry of leading a church that might be struggling to build numbers. For some chaplains, but not all, income might be slightly higher and so family finances can become easier.

* * *

The names have been changed but the examples above are based on true incidents. The rest of this chapter will consist of three reflections that may help Henrietta as she faces the question raised earlier: How will she cope with her change in role, with these contrasting views about what she is doing providing an uncertain backdrop?

Three thoughts are offered:

Watching one's spiritual life.
Learning from desert life.
Enjoying incarnational life.

Keeping the flame alive

In Paul's farewell to the Ephesian leaders (Acts 20), he called upon them to 'watch themselves'. Transition to chaplaincy, like any change, needs to include a careful guarding and cherishing of spiritual life.

The normal markers of spiritual discipline have been taken away. It may be difficult to say the liturgical offices at the same time or in the same sort of building as before. The chaplain may need to develop a new rhythm of prayer, sacrament, fellowship and Bible study. The rhythm of the week and year can feel different. Festivals such as Christmas may be celebrated twice, once at work and once at church. There may be a requirement to be supportive of the festivals of other faiths, and certainly to be sensitive and alert to those faiths, and to members of the community who do not follow a religious faith at all.

Chaplains can indeed be marginalized but some are rather too good at marginalizing themselves. Worryingly, they do not join a local church, they ignore diocesan mailings and they do not join local and national chaplaincy networks. There needs to be the discipline of genuine commitment to a mutually supportive fellowship.

There will be questions of time and money to be faced. For chaplains in education there may be the need to develop two rhythms of spiritual discipline, one for term time and one for holidays. If income has gone up (and it is an 'if', remuneration for some chaplaincies is lower than the overall housing and stipend package for parish clergy), there will be the spiritual challenge of having a higher income.

A useful checklist for Henrietta will continue to be the questions asked of her at ordination, and perhaps especially these:

Will you be diligent in prayer, in reading Holy Scripture, and in all studies that will deepen your faith and fit you to bear witness to the truth of the gospel?

Will you work with your fellow servants in the gospel for the sake of the kingdom of God?

Will you endeavour to fashion your own life and that of your household according to the way of Christ, that you may be a pattern and example to Christ's people?

Remembering that deserts are important places in Christian thinking

For some ministers the move to chaplaincy feels like the beginning of a journey into a wilderness; they are being called away from the usual structures and conversations that dominate church thinking. Their identity as a parish priest has been given up and it may be unclear what remains. It is not true 'wilderness', where all is stripped away, but it is certainly *different*.

After the affirmation of his baptism Jesus goes to the wilderness. At the heart of the narrative of Jesus's experience in the desert is the identity question: 'If you are the Son of God ...?' or, to put it another way: 'What does it mean to be you?'

We note three points from this narrative:

1. Jesus brought with him to the desert the knowledge that God loved him and had a purpose for him. He is the beloved son, he has words to say that are to be heard. Similarly, a chaplain still has the affirmation of God's Church through ordination, and still carries the Church's commission. The Ordinal is not a job description for parish or chaplaincy ministry, it is a calling and commissioning to be an ordained minister of the Church of England, whatever the context. The new chaplain is loved by God and commissioned by the Church as much when serving in a hospital as when she was in a parish.

2. Jesus brought a deep understanding of Scripture to his new context. The tempter quoted Scripture but misused it. In all times, but especially in times of change, it is important to read the Scriptures thoughtfully and humbly, being mindful of the big themes of the character and purposes of God.

3. Sometimes a new chaplain may be tempted to make a splash in his or her new role, to make their mark quickly, to establish a new significance for them. For Jesus there were the temptations to short-cut the wilderness experience by turning stone to bread, to do something spectacular to get himself noticed, to offer his worship in the wrong direction to gain supposed authority and prestige. It is wise for the new chaplain to focus on the essentials of loving God and loving one's neighbour, and to remember the importance of patience and faith. God will be at work; seeds sometimes take time to grow, things need not be rushed. The noisy and spectacular may be our agenda rather than God's.

Jesus understood his identity, what he was called to do and how he was called to do it. He resisted the temptations, resting instead on his understanding of the nature of God as revealed in the Scriptures, and with the 'this is my beloved son' still ringing in his ears.

Henrietta may also consider another scriptural desert experience.

In Acts 8, Philip, fresh from an unexpected and fruitful ministry in Samaria, which followed a recognized and exciting (if brief) season as one of the seven deacons in Jerusalem, finds himself on a desert road. Alone. A modern strategist might have kept Philip in Samaria (how must the growing community of believers have felt when he left?) and not placed him in the middle of nowhere. But a higher strategist was at work, and soon the chariot carrying the Ethiopian comes trundling by.

Before he heard the chariot wheels, did Philip look back wistfully to his previous ministries? Did he wonder what was going on? A chaplain does not choose whom she serves. Occasionally there are churches where the congregation and the vicar have chosen each other; this can happen quite subtly over a number of years, where the unspoken 'people like us' rule of membership has grown strong. In contrast, the chaplain has no control over the intake of those among whom he or she ministers; there is no knowing who will be in the next chariot that passes by.

(And the 'passing by' is a feature of this ministry. Many of the community will be moving on each year.)

And she may remember, and be encouraged by, church history. Often words of insight and wisdom have been spoken into church life by those in the desert, physically or metaphorically. Chaplaincy has been a growth area in the Church in recent decades. Perhaps these growing voices from the margins, from this mission field, may yet be of significance in the transformation and renewal of the Church of England.

Christ-like ministry is incarnational ministry

Henrietta loves being with people. The Church may have 'set her apart' for ordained ministry but that does not mean for her that she is set apart from other people. Quite the opposite: she wants to be with them. As a school chaplain Henrietta gets over-busy writing reports, as others do. She uses the same toilets. Eats at the same tables. Shares the same jokes and tears. The conversations are spread over days, months and years. She is on show all the time, in the dining hall, classroom and on the sports field. Her behaviour counts as much as the assemblies she gives. The fruit of the Spirit needs to be truly there; this is close-range ministry and people will not be fooled by cardboard cut-outs. Chaplaincy is rather like the idealized vision of old-fashioned parish ministry: the parson as member of, and priest to, the village. Henrietta bumps into people continually. She shares the pressured, tragic and joyful times of the year, not as an observer but as a true member of a community, on equal terms with everyone else. She knows everyone and is there for everyone, of whatever faith or none.

The student and Henrietta emerge from different classrooms into the same corridor. 'I've been meaning to ask you,' the student asks, 'what did Jesus really think about the Old Testament?' A colleague quizzes her about the latest church scandal. Another looks shell-shocked after a difficult meeting with a parent. A student finds her to hand in his homework: 'Oh, and Miss, do you have to be baptized to go to heaven?' Another looks round the door: 'At what age can I refuse to see my father under custody arrangements?' Henrietta arrives back in her room to find a girl who does not want to speak at all, but simply wants silence and space. A member of the catering staff brings in photos of her new granddaughter. Intellectually and spiritually Henrietta has to be ready all the time. There are very few spaces during the working day.

It can be very intense and fast-moving. Henrietta needs to remember that each of these people, adult or pupil, is loved and valued as they are, made in the image of God. Christians believe that God so loved the *world* that Jesus came and that the birth of Christ is announced as good news for '*all the people*'. And she is with hundreds of representatives of *all the people*, not just ones who think the same as she does, every day.

A key part of the calling is indeed the building up of the faithful in their discipleship; there is the challenge of working with, and leading, Christians of different backgrounds. It is important to find the right books, words and prayers to help them grow. The chaplain is there to serve, not to impose a particular churchmanship style.

But most of a chaplain's time is likely to be spent with non-Christians. As a parish priest you are usually with people who want to be with you, or at least are willing to be with you while weddings or funerals are arranged. As a chaplain you are probably with rather a lot of people who feel no desire or need to be with an ordained person at all. They have to put up with you and, equally importantly, the chaplain has to learn to minister to them.

There might be a tangential question here about ordained

ministry in some parishes and in the structures of the Church. Eugene Peterson, in *The Contemplative Pastor*, writes powerfully about the ease with which ministers can lose sight of their ministerial calling and end up running an organization instead.[3] (Often lay people are far better at running organizations than clergy, but our over-clericalized Church tends to hide that truth.) A retired vicar once said: 'I feel I am now a true priest again, having time to minister to people instead of chairing meetings.' Perhaps we need to work harder to free up parish clergy to do what they were ordained to do. Perhaps similar discussions should happen with diocesan posts – how much of this job description genuinely requires an ordained person? What can be taken out and shared round the Body of Christ? Historically, revival has come when those called to ministry have exercised ministry and not been distracted or drawn away. An experienced and senior priest said to a young school chaplain, 'This is a good calling for you, I believe you have a gift of evangelism.' This was encouraging for the chaplain, but it is a gift that surely should be yearned for by all who have responded to the ordinal question:

Will you lead Christ's people in proclaiming his glorious gospel, so that the good news of salvation may be heard in every place?

It is vital that we equip others to do it, but it is strange if we are not also doing it ourselves. Chaplains encourage Christians but are equally on the front line themselves. The same should be true of every ordained minister in the Church of England, from curate to Archbishop (and present and recent Archbishops have been particularly good at this).

The phrase 'incarnational ministry' has deliberate echoes of Christ's incarnation and this includes the priority of service. Jesus said: 'Now that I, your Lord and Teacher, have washed your feet, you also should wash one another's feet. I have set you an example that you should do as I have done for you' (John 13.14–15).

There was no glamour or status in taking off the outer garment and of washing feet at the end of a busy day. There will be countless opportunities for Henrietta to serve others: from assisting at the bedside of the dying to holding doors open in corridors, from driving the school minibus to covering a lesson for a tired colleague. It will not be glamorous but it will be expressing the servant love of Christ.

Henrietta is not only called to serve the community she is part of; she is equally called to serve the Church. It is encouraging that some dioceses are increasingly using the skills that chaplains have developed. One school chaplain was recently asked by his diocese to help with the teaching and mentoring of curates. Like all ministers, chaplains have qualities and gifts that can be a blessing to the wider Church.

Conclusion

The three reflections above may be of use to Henrietta and others moving from parish to chaplaincy. But she may wish simply to reflect on the words of Martin Luther King who said, in a sermon delivered on 4 February 1968 that was played at his funeral later that year:

> There is deep down within all of us an instinct. It's a kind of drum major instinct – a desire to be out front, a desire to lead the parade, a desire to be first ...
>
> But that isn't what Jesus did; he did something altogether different. He said in substance ... 'Keep feeling the need for being first. But I want you to be first in love. I want you to be first in moral excellence. I want you to be first in generosity. That is what I want you to do.'

Henrietta is seeking to serve God and his people, wherever they may be found. She is trying to obey her calling to the vital and growing ministry of chaplaincy, despite sometimes being misunderstood by the Church that she loves. Perhaps King's threefold reference point is a good place to begin as she copes with these contrasting emotions.

First in love.
First in moral excellence.
First in generosity.

Parish ministry and chaplaincy are equally exciting, challenging and satisfying. It is an honour to serve in either. It will be a good day for the Church of England when both are seen equally as part of God's plan for the growth of the kingdom, and when it is easy for people to move between the two if that is their calling, knowing that experience in one can bless the other.

As I write this last paragraph I note that I have been privileged to be involved in over a hundred pastoral and spiritual conversations in the last week. Any of these would have been moving or encouraging to recount but it seems fitting to mention two separate conversations with 17-year-olds about vocation to ordained ministry. I initiated one of these, the young man went very quiet and then said, 'For the first time in my life that thought came into my head last night, and now you have mentioned it today.' The other was started by the student himself; it had been on his mind for some time and he wanted to tell someone and a school chaplain seemed a good place to begin. Please pray for these two young people, for our schools and indeed all our places of work. And for those called to be chaplains to these communities. It is all rather exciting.

Moving from parish to chaplaincy – questions to consider

- Have I discussed and checked my own motives in moving from parish to chaplaincy, and have I communicated them properly to others?
- In making a change from parochial to sector ministry, what am I missing and why am I missing it?
- How do I keep my personal pattern of prayer, Bible-reading and fellowship flourishing when I am in a different pattern of ministry?
- What do I like about incarnational ministry, and what do I find difficult?
- How can I best exercise my responsibility to the local and wider church?
- What is exciting about chaplaincy?

Notes

1. Miranda Threlfall-Holmes and Mark Newitt, *Being a Chaplain*, London: SPCK, 2011, p. 138.

2. Threlfall-Holmes and Newitt, *Being a Chaplain*, p. 138.

3. Eugene H. Peterson, *The Contemplative Pastor*, Grand Rapids: Eerdmans, 1993.

9

Letting Go and Holding On

VIV THOMAS

After considerable thought, prayer, conversation, excitement and anxiety, my wife and I decided to leave the south London church we were leading and head towards Pakistan. The spark which ignited the idea in the first place was a rejection by other leaders of a particular initiative which I thought essential and they did not. Anyway, all things considered it was time to go. Our last Sunday in the church was memorable. We said farewell at three meetings and one of them was the Sunday school. With 120 children and many teachers present we were called out to be prayed for. As people were praying, one of the teachers started to cry, and within a few seconds tears began to roll down my face. Before long many of the children were crying. Questions flooded into my head. Was I betraying these children? How could I leave and make children cry? What sort of pastor was I to so upset children? To me this was a demonstration of how these people and crying children were going to miss me. At the end of Sunday school my wife and I took two sisters home in our car. The sisters were about seven years old. As they got into the back seat they started to cry some more. Before we pulled away and with my guilt increasing, I turned around and asked them if they were going to be all right. Quietly they said yes. Then through her tears one of them shattered my image of what was going on when she blurted out, 'Pastor ... my rabbit's dead' and through more tears her sister said, 'Now we can get a dog', and more tears rolled down their faces. A little stunned I turned back and looked through the front windscreen. I thought they were crying about my departure and the chasm that was going to open up in their lives once I had moved on. It was not so. They had felt the emotion in the Sunday school and filled it with their own meaning. Sadly, it was not about me but about rabbits, dogs and whatever else was popping into children's minds when they saw grown people blubbering in public.

This can be the nature of leadership transitions. You often don't know what is going on in yourself or others. Working out what God is doing can be even more difficult. It is also problematic to read the events and changing landscapes of our lives while seeking to work out what they mean. This is what makes transitions so tricky.

To what do we need to pay attention as we go through these times of leadership transition? I want to articulate two critical biblical themes, engage two Scripture passages and draw two conclusions that should help and bring perspective.

Theme one: Living the story

Every church and every leader has a story. How fruitful that church and leader become connected to how well their story relates to the story of God. Scripture marks out that story, moving us from Genesis to Revelation or from creation to a new heaven and earth. Creation, fall, Israel, incarnation, redemption, ascension, Church and future hope outline the overwhelming and mighty themes of Scripture. The more our churches and leaders are rooted in each part of that biblical story, the more fully alive they will be and the more glory God will have. Irenaeus taught us this. For in the end the only thing that matters is the Trinity and the kingdom of God. The story of Father, Son and Holy Spirit and what God is doing in the world through establishing the kingdom is told in the story of Scripture. If we neglect part of that huge narrative and become selective in the areas we think are preferable, a price will have to be paid sooner or later. In other words, if we do not take Scripture seriously both in developing church culture and our own lives as leaders we will be bamboozled in ministry and particularly in times of ministry transition.

Let me illustrate. If you, as a leader, neglect the story of the fall and therefore miss the nature of your own sinful rebellious heart, it becomes very difficult to access reality. Accessing reality is a critical responsibility for a leader. If the story of the fall is neglected or underplayed you can easily misread yourself. Having done that, it is then much more difficult to discern what is happening around you. Skimming over the story of the fall will lead you to becoming the victim of your own eccentric biases because you will not have been able to track the true nature of your own heart. It is the Holy Spirit who gives us awareness of our broken lives in a broken world, granting us the humility to enter into glorious acts of refreshing repentance. When we repent and submit ourselves to God and what he is doing in the world, our judgement and our discernment return, or at least have the chance to.

On the other hand, if you miss the future hope ahead and fail to anticipate what Miroslav Volf calls our 'eschatological maximum', another price is to be paid.[1] The world becomes small and you fail to make decisions in the light of the huge future intentions of God. It is only in the light of an anticipation of a new heaven and new earth that we can come to an understanding of what has happened in our lives and what is happening as we pass through times of transition. Leaders stumble when they do not have this future hope setting their hearts on fire when developing strategies and forging church cultures. Another cost of underplaying this part of the story is loss of patience. If you are leading without a rich anticipation of the future of God, it is much more difficult to delay the gratifications of success that leadership often offers. Misread the future and misunderstand the present.

To flourish through times of transition we need to live the story of God and not just particular parts of the story we prefer. All the lenses of the story need to be lined up adequately so we can see as clearly as possible the place where we find ourselves, the transition we are in and what could be the way forward in the future.

Theme two: Permanent transition

Walter Bruggemann explains how the Psalms work and in doing so explains how life and spiritual leadership work. He puts everything in a context of transition. He identifies three movements through which we all move.[2] He divides up the Psalms into three divisions: psalms of orientation, psalms of disorientation and psalms of new orientation. David G. Firth,[3] picking up on Brueggemann, renames these divisions as Psalms of the ordered world, the disordered world and reordered world. All the Psalms are intended to be prayed as we go through these various stages of life. Ordered is when life is where we want it to be. Disordered usually describes what happens soon after we think it is ordered. Reordered is when through God's work and word a fresh position is established and we feel ordered again. The idea is permanent transition both in our conversation with God and in how we engage with life in the everyday.

This is how leadership in general, and spiritual leadership in particular, work. We think all is under control and we are doing well. Then some wave hits us and the ship begins to roll, challenging the course we have set. Then as Captain we take corrective measures and equilibrium is established until another wave hits or the weather system changes, bringing a new set of issues and decisions. I don't think there is another alternative to this model when it comes to spiritual leadership or maybe any type of leadership. This is the way it will be because we are forever engaging particular persons, fresh conditions and our own complex lives as we seek to lead people forward. We are on a continual journey through order, disorder and reorder even if we never move home or church. The only issue is the intensity of the shifting sea and the particular weather system we are living through at the time.[4]

Realizing that we are in a place of permanent change is critical in doing well in specific leadership transitions. Perhaps the illusion is to imagine that we are ever in a safe place of orientation, order and stability where nothing alters when in fact the world is swirling around us all of the time and we are in continual change. The time of transition from one church responsibility to another is just a change in the nature of the transition we face continually. Ralph D. Stacey explains, 'continuing movement towards equilibrium is a failure; success requires the maintenance of a position away from equilibrium'.[5] Perhaps he has read the Psalms. The truth is that everything is in transition all of the time, be it at glacial pace or tsunami thunder. It is going to be challenging to adapt to transitions and change unless we work with these categories of order, disorder and reorder in one form or another throughout the whole of our lives. The Psalms are key texts for leaders in transition because they are the praises, prayers and complaints of leaders who have gone through it before us.

Story one: Jesus at Nazareth

Transition was intended in Nazareth. The shifting relationship between the leader and the led – or in Nazareth's case the not to be led – is starkly explained in Mark 6.1–6. This is how I see the story. Jesus and the disciples arrived in Nazareth which was his home town. Before long the relational and organizational distance between Jesus and the people of Nazareth became apparent. Things had clearly changed. This was not only home town for Jesus, it was also small town because Nazareth would not face the big world Jesus was opening before their eyes. It seemed that the people of Nazareth could not adjust to what they saw in front of them. Jesus was the boy to them but now he was returning as the man or, even worse, a leader. It appears his transformation had outstripped their ability to adapt to what he now was. Jesus even had a following of disciples and assistants. Home town Nazareth appeared struggled with this. You can hear the relational gears grinding and jamming together as Nazareth tried to work out what was in front of them and who this Jesus was now.

Nazareth failed to navigate the transition in a healthy way. They preferred their unbelief. It seems like it was all too much for them to grasp. Many were amazed at Jesus's teaching but others – or the same people – took offence at him. It is as though they were paralysed in the middle of the road as the twin headlights of his wisdom and miracles bore down on them. They asked the questions, 'Isn't this the carpenter? Isn't this Mary's son and the brother of James, Joseph, Judas and Simon? Aren't his sisters here with us?' (Mark 6.3). It could also be that they just decided to be offended, therefore gifting themselves a way out of dealing with the stunning realities of what was happening through Jesus. If he was what his life demonstrated then the people of Nazareth had deep challenges to face and new thoughts to think. The implications were immense.

How did they resolve this internal conflict they endured? Who can know the exact motivations of the people of Nazareth? Yet, boxing Jesus up seemed to be the solution. It appears that they needed to put Jesus into a box so they could manage him. They were not aware that the box was ridiculously small and was destined to be shattered by the resurrection. We have in Nazareth a community that could not cope with the transition of a boy becoming a man and a follower becoming a leader. The people of Nazareth had congealed into their final selves and little could be done. Nazareth refused to be mentored by the one they nurtured. It seems that they could not cope with a prophet who to them was a little boy. Their inability to change amazed Jesus, and rather than it being described as an adjustment problem or some other minor weakness, he described it in much more challenging language as a 'lack of faith' (Mark 6.6).

Story two: Peter and Cornelius

In contrast to the people of Nazareth are Peter and Cornelius. Their story of transition is explained in Acts 10. Cornelius was a centurion in the Italian Regiment. He was devout, God-fearing and generous. He lived in Caesarea, the Roman capital over Judea. He would have been leading up to 600 men in his Roman cohort who were probably archers. Cornelius would have worked his way up through the ranks being a non-commissioned officer.[6] He was helpful to the poor and had healthy prayer habits. Yet, he was a non-Jew leading an army of occupation. He may well have been sympathetic to Judaism, but he was not a follower of Christ until a meeting happened in his house. Cornelius prayed at three o'clock in the afternoon and had a vision of an angel. The messenger spoke Cornelius's name and filled him with fear while telling him to go and get Simon Peter. Cornelius sent three of his men to complete the task.

Ministry transitions do not come with much greater intensity than the one God offered Peter through his roof-top vision and the obedient response of Cornelius. We know Peter well. Here is the courageous walk-on-water Apostle. He was a devout Jew and now leader in the emerging Church. God had used him wonderfully, particularly after the resurrection and the outpouring of the Holy Spirit. He was in the beautiful place of Joppa, which is now Jaffa, part of coastal Tel Aviv. He went up onto his roof to pray. In prayer he had a trance and a vision was given to him. For a Jew this would have been a horrific vision. On a sheet lowered down from heaven came four-footed animals, reptiles and birds. Then a voice said, 'Get up Peter, kill and eat.' He replied, 'Surely not Lord!' Peter received this vision three times. This is not the first time Peter had to hear something three times.

While Peter was hesitating, doing his 'wondering' and 'thinking', he found that God had provided some leverage that gave Peter momentum. A Roman soldier and his servants were outside his house just as the Spirit had said. Peter was now in significant transition. His visionary trance was changing into concrete reality. This experience was now very real and standing in front of him in the shape of three men calling out his name. The centurion's messengers wanted Peter to come and speak to them at Cornelius's house in Caesarea. Peter's world was being inverted and transformed yet he responded positively to this request.

Peter went through his normal prayer routine and his ethical-theological world was shattered in this place of prayer. He was a Jew and was restricted in what he could eat (Lev. 11). In his vision were clean and unclean animals and it scandalized him. Yet, this was also a staggering vision of future Jew and Gentile relationships to be expressed in the future Church. Peter was being introduced to the unthinkable because of the new thing God was doing through Cornelius. This was not only Peter receiving fresh vision, it was a picture of the future shape of the worldwide Church. Peter said, 'It is against our law for a Jew to associate with Gentiles or even visit them' (10.28) but that is precisely what he was doing. Up to this point the Apostle was a religious sectarian but now he had the radical challenges of spectacular transition pressing against his nose. God had just shown him that no race is better than another. Nothing was ever going to be the same again for Peter or for the Church.

Cornelius and Peter were both on a journey towards each other, a journey that Peter would find very difficult. But it is Peter's ability to be shaped by Cornelius that helps change him and in the end changes the world. If Peter had not made that transition the gospel could have been locked up for years in some sectarian scheme and never broken out into the Gentile world.

What can we take from these two themes and passages when it comes to ministry transitions? What should shape our imaginations from these themes and passages? I want to focus on two areas.

Becoming accomplished in living out of control

I have always enjoyed my times of ministry transition. They have always been fresh places of thought and release but this is not so for many. Each of us has to find the grace, imagination, revelation and practice to find our own way through.

One of the reasons why ministry transitions can be so challenging is because we feel vulnerable and out of control for as long as they last. The time of transition is the time of disconnection where everything is being shifted from one place to another. This theme of living out of control is summed up by the ever quotable Stanley Hauerwas who writes, 'Learning to live out of control, learning to live without trying to force contingency into conformity because of our desperate need for security, I take as a resource for discovering alternatives that would otherwise not be present.'[7] Eugene H. Peterson expresses much the same thing in his writing.[8] If we are able to let go of the controls of our lives, who knows what blessings may come our way that we would not otherwise have noticed if we had kept control. As Christian ministers and leaders we are not living our own story. We cannot live as if we are the sole producers of our own lives. Rather, living out of control, yet rooted in the middle of the story of God opens up our imaginations to all the possibilities offered in times of transition. We cannot control the various events and seasons which come to us as we move through order, disorder and reorder. What we can control is our response to them.

Peter was able to live out of control but the people of Nazareth were not. It was as Peter responded to his vision that revelation happened. Significant breakthrough took place in his imagination and world view as he responded to the vision when he merged back into the material reality of Joppa after his trance. Peter explained later that, through his vision, inaccurate and inappropriate judgements were challenged, 'God has shown me that I should not call anyone impure or unclean' (9.28) and his parochial local world became global, 'God does not show favouritism but accepts those from every nation who fear him and do right' (9.35). This only came to him as he was willing to go with the startling vision of what God was calling him to do and live out of control. Yet, it is remarkable how many Christian leaders, called to follow Jesus wherever he leads, can be so controlling when the process of transition takes place. My guess is that fear quietly injects itself into our hearts and solidifies in our heads so we can't think straight.

Here is a challenge, for this is where we are called to be exemplars. How can we call people to a life of faith and risk if we cannot be schooled in learning to live out of control, which is a prerequisite of the life of faith? It is so easy to be seduced by our own expectations of the institution or denomination for which we work and imagine that it must carry us or always find a place for us. For some it is as though there is a debt to be paid to us by our institution or denomination. We feel we are owed even though these same organizations have given us a place to live out our calling. With this sense of being owed worming around our heads we trust the institution to deliver rather than the God in whom we trust. Never confuse the Church of England with the Holy Trinity, the two are not identical. Fifteen years ago I took a sabbatical from a group I was working with. While I was considering the move, one of the leaders said to me, 'Don't do it, you will lose your powerbase if you go.' I took this as another confirmation that it was time to take the sabbatical. Grasping and clinging on to institutional power will make transitions particularly difficult. To flourish through transition we need to learn to let go. Peter could do this. Nazareth could not.

Walking through transition with others

We are being shaped and mentored in one way or another. All of our assumptions around how life works and our understanding of common sense demonstrate the influence of culture, family and relationships. We are being formed through our choices and what they come to mean for us. Right at the heart of this formation is the company we have kept and now keep. 'Do not be deceived' says Paul, 'God cannot be mocked. People reap what they sow' (Gal. 67). Our ability to cope with times of transition will be related to the company we have kept before the transition takes place. Who have been the people who have shaped our hearts and minds?

For pastors and church leaders times of transition are intensely related to people. The work of being a pastor or shepherd means that times of departure and transition are full of emotional, spiritual and psychological fissures. There are high expectations emotionally, spiritually and psychologically when re-engaging with the next group of people we are called to lead. Moving on in ministry is to do with pastoral responsibility being handed over to someone else and picking up a new set of responsibilities from another once the time of transition has ended.[9]

Right at the core of ministry transition is mentoring. What ideas have mentored me? What desires mentor me? Who is mentoring me through this transition process? Who am I mentoring? Where am I rooted in my head and heart as the transition takes place? We cannot know ourselves alone. Without community to teach us who we are, we are lost in a desert of introspection and guesswork. Walking through ministry transition with others is vital to doing it well. I want to identify three areas of mentoring which will help as we navigate ministry transition.

Mentored by God

Jim Houston explains what a Christian is through stating, 'Becoming a Christian is a demolition of one's identity from the ruins of self-enclosure as being individualistic – literally 'in-human' –

whereas to be human is to be a social being. Instead, one becomes more 'open', not only to other people, but also to become radically reconstituted as a 'person-in-Christ'.[10] Becoming a Christian is to do with the shift from just being self-defined, self-focused and individual to becoming a 'person' who becomes who they are because of their communion with God and their community with other people.

Understanding ourself as a 'person' in this sense is central to ministry and leadership transitions and to great spiritual leadership. This is at the core of what God is doing in our lives and is our deepest need. Kierkegaard taught us that a human being's highest achievement is to let God be able to help him (or her). In one sentence he resets the cultural clock of the Western world and explains to us what human success looks like. Success is being mentored by God in relationship with Father, Son and Holy Spirit.

Therefore, right at the heart of leadership transitions are the practices and disciplines of the faith, and in particular prayer. Scripture is also central to the process. Reading Scripture not only for information but for formation shapes the way in which we respond to God, the world and ourselves. A prayerful contemplative engagement with Scripture nourishes us on the journey during times of transition. It was in the place of prayer that Peter was mentored by God through receiving his vision and a whole new world opened up for him. His ordered world became disordered but was reordered as he listened to God.

If God does not mentor us through Scripture and prayer then we will be mentored by other things which will shape our heads and hearts. Money, sex, power, fear, time and place will tend to dominate and enslave our decision-making processes during times of change. Being mentored through Scripture and in prayer by Father, Son and Holy Spirit will keep us nourished and receptive in times of transition and able to spot the serpent's tail.

Mentored by community

In contemporary Western organizational life mentoring is usually seen as a dialogue between two people. The idea is that someone who is a bit further along the road helps someone just beginning the journey. We have many examples of this in Scripture with Elisha and Elijah, Ruth and Naomi, Barnabas and Paul, Paul and almost everyone else in the New Testament. But the weight of the mentoring process needs to be communal rather than one-on-one relationships, important as they are.

Jesus developed his disciples in community. He called the group into existence and formed it around himself as the teacher. The motivation behind his mentoring was not to discover the potential of each disciple so they could live their lives well or that they may have a sense of fulfilment. They were called together so they may establish the Church. Jesus calls, teaches, walks with and releases his disciples so they will become the leaders of the emerging Church. This communal mentoring theme continues into the first centuries of the Church. Cyprian, Pachomius, Basil of Caesarea, and Augustine all place an emphasis on mentoring the group and not only the individual.[11] However, keeping good company in communal mentoring is important. If you were mentored by the Nazareth community it would have been a toxic experience. Keeping the right company is critical when it comes to shaping our imaginations and the decisions we make. However, keeping the right company does not mean keeping safe company.

I have been the member of several mentoring groups. Some have been built around a leader and some have been more peer-focused. The relationships built up in these groups often survive after the conclusion of the group. Many of these sorts of groups go on for decades. These relationships are vital at times of ministry transition. They often contain people who love you but are not so interested in what you can do for them or the particular ministry you have. They usually contain people who are more interested in you as a person rather than in what you can deliver. This is what makes them valuable, particularly in times of transition. They are particularly helpful in absorbing the shock of change and in working out the possible options for the future.

Mentored by a person

If you are blessed you may also have a person who is your mentor, this is a person who 'with God-given capacity and God-given responsibility to influence a specific group of God's people towards His purposes for the group',[12] mentors you. Church leadership is to do with influencing a group towards God but in times of transition those same leaders usually need someone to mentor them.

A skilled mentor is able to notice our story and see how it connects or disconnects with the story of God. They are able to challenge us and call us out of our self-indulgence and fantasies so we may re-engage with God's story. They are often able to notice where we are in terms of order, disorder and reorder, sometimes pointing out that what we considered to be disorder is actually reordering or what we considered as order needs some disordering. They can become Cornelius-like figures in our lives obediently responding to God's initiative and preventing us from developing Nazareth-like stubbornness when called by God to change. A good mentor leads us out of our boxed-up lives and points out the horizons and possibilities ahead. In doing so they prepare us for the next phase of ministry and pastoral responsibility when we will do the same thing for others who are negotiating their way through the labyrinth of money, sex, power, time and place.

Living the story of God, allowing room for our reordering, disavowing the unbelief of Nazareth and being open to the voice of God are cultivated in us as we learn to live out of control and experience a mentored life. At least this is what I have learned on the journey so far. What is the one virtue that brings this together? Courage. We will need the courage to say no to a little life and yes to the biggest life we can possibly live. If we have the title of minister, leader, pastor or shepherd, our calling demands no less. All this is preparation for the time when a weeping little girl bursts your vain imaginings by telling you, 'Pastor ... my rabbit's dead', and introduces you to the realities of ministry transition.

Notes

1. See Volf, Miroslav, *After Our Likeness: The Church as the Image of the Trinity*, Grand Rapids: Wm. B. Eerdmans, 1998, p. 199: 'if the church attempts to live at a "historical minimum" she misses the possibilities God has given her. If she attempts to live with a "statically understood maximum" she risks missing her historical reality through sliding into ideology.'

2. Walter Brueggemann, *The Message of the Psalms*, Minneapolis: Augsburg, 1984.

3. David G. Firth, *Hear, O Lord: A Spirituality of the Psalms*, Cliff College Publishing, 2005.

4. It is possible to live through all of these phases at one time, depending on the various spheres of life we inhabit.

5. Ralph C. Stacey, *Strategic Management and Organisational Dynamics*, Pitman Publishing, 1993.

6. Frank E. Gaebelein (ed.), *The Expositor's Bible Commentary*, Vol. 9, Grand Rapids: Zondervan, 1981: Richard N. Longenecker, *Acts*, Zondervan, 1995, p. 385.

7. Stanley Hauerwas, *Hannah's Child,* London: SCM Press, 2010, p. 137.

8. Eugene H. Peterson, *The Jesus Way*, London: Hodder, 2007, p. 276, where Peterson describes Hauerwas as 'my theologian of choice as a conversation partner'.

9. The intensity of this process depends much on the model, style and ecclesiology practised. In more collegial models this transition can be easier but it depends on what is really happening underneath the skin of the church and leadership.

10. James H. Houston, *The Mentored Life: From Individualism to Personhood*, Nav Press, 2002.

11. Edward L. Smither, *Augustine and Mentor: A Model for Preparing Spiritual Leaders*, Nashville: B&H Publishing, 2008, pp. 90–91. Smither also points out the importance of correspondence and Church Councils as critical mentoring tackle.

12. Robert Clinton, *The Making of a Leader*, Colorado Springs: Nave Press, 1988, p. 245.

IO

Affirmation and Accountability: Moving On Through Ministerial Development Review

HAZEL WHITEHEAD

It seems to me that these are the two key words which determine the rationale for clergy review; or, to put it another way, they are the twin pillars on which it is founded. *Affirmation and Accountability* is the title of a report which investigated the problem of rising numbers of incidents of clergy stress.[1] This report was seminal for me as I was responsible for revising and implementing the Bishop of Guildford's Review scheme in the light of the Ecclesiastical Offices (Terms of Service) Regulations 2009.[2] In ministerial life, says the Report:

> There is fundamentally a two-way bargain: clergy desperately need more affirmation ... the other side ... is the need to be open to much greater accountability.

It suggested, among other things, that by giving proper care and attention to review and continuing training, and by both affirming clergy and holding them to account, the Church might make a positive contribution to clergy health and well-being and, in addition, benefit the wider Church. An enhanced Ministerial Development Review process would be one tool in the process and might even be a catalyst for transformation of ministerial experience.[3]

But by whom should clergy be affirmed and to whom are they accountable? Why should they *need* to be affirmed or held to account? Surely following a vocation in ordained ministry is reward enough; and aren't all clergy conscientious and hardworking? My experience of 18 years' involvement in training and nurturing ministers makes me want to say yes – and no – to the last two questions. Our Director of Ordinands often says 'I don't have a job. I have a life', and this positive spin means that he sees his life and ministry as one, and as an offering to God. However, for some clergy life can be fragmented, lonely, pressurized, frustrating and exhausting. Rather like Sisyphus, condemned to roll a boulder up a hill only to see it roll down again, the interminable daily, weekly and annual cycle of liturgy, visiting, administration, occasional offices, parochial arguments and endless new national or diocesan ventures can take the edge off the excitement and spiritual uplift which comes with ordination. So vocation may not be reward enough. Clergy are, after all, only human. They need diocesan, as well as local, encouragement.

They also need to be held to account. A minority may need to be taken to task over serious issues but holding to account does not necessarily imply discipline or serious criticism. Faithful and diligent clergy sometimes need to be challenged about overworking or how they prioritize their activities, or need to be nudged into a change of direction, jolted out of complacency or encouraged to use their gifts more generously. All this must be done within a pastoral framework. We know that clergy inhabit a difficult place. They are expected to be self-motivated and self-critical, under authority and yet responsible for their own performance. Few have proper supervision because there is no accessible 'line manager' and they must balance their own gifts and preferences with the requirements of their context and calling. Under the new 'Terms of Service' they are encouraged to have a role description for a role that defies easy description. So there are underlying complexities. Furthermore, longer-serving clergy suffer from the mixed economy of past and present. They have fond memories of a friendly chat by the bishop's fire during which the bishop might ask, cajole or persuade the clergyman to move. For some of them – thankfully an ever decreasing minority – review is just an irritating, paper-driven intrusion or the infiltration of dubious, commercial or business practices into spiritual affairs. In contrast, others, and especially those who have come from other professions, take it all in their stride and appreciate its benefits. Clergy are not all the same, so one size does not fit all – but they have the same foundational ordination liturgy in common. What were their expectations and those of the Church as they embarked on the priestly task?

The Ordinal

We might imagine that affirmation is deeply embedded in the liturgy and, implicitly, it is; but there is far more which speaks of accountability. At the point of ordination, clergy profess that they will be loyal to the Queen, 'pay due and canonical obedience to the bishop' and give heed to the canons of the Church. The bishop declares that priests are to:

> proclaim the word of the Lord ... watch for the signs of God's new creation ... be messengers, watchmen and stewards of the Lord ... teach and admonish, feed and provide for his family, search for his (God's) children in the wilderness of his world's temptations ... guide them through its confusions ... call hearers to repentance ... declare absolution ... baptize ... nurture ... unfold the scriptures ... preside at the Lord's table ... lead worship ... minister to the sick and dying.

Not surprisingly, the bishop continues, 'We trust that long ago you began to ponder all this ...' Lest the potential priest is in any doubt about the enormity of the task, a set of challenges follows for which the response is 'By the help of God, I will' or something similar. The bishop bids the candidates '... remember the greatness of the trust that is now to be committed to your charge' and that 'It is to him (Christ) that you will render account for your stewardship of his people.'

There is no doubt that, from the outset, the demands of ministry are challenging and perhaps the Ordinal alone (rather than legislation) should persuade us of the efficacy of review. Obedience is not an optional extra but a foundational characteristic of what it means to be ordained – and clergy may need to be reminded of this when they come for review.

The annual ordination services lead seamlessly into a process of support and review. In Guildford Diocese, we already took our review process seriously but new legislation made us re-evaluate whether it was fit for purpose in the new age of *Common Tenure*.[4] In looking for ways to help clergy identify the positive benefits of review, we decided to investigate whether there was a theological rationale underlying it. If we could root the process in Scripture and our shared Christian heritage, perhaps it could be allowed to become both a vehicle through which the Spirit speaks and a creative opportunity to enhance ministry. This needed to be thought about more carefully.

Reflecting theologically

When I was a young Christian, I used to think about life and wonder where God fitted in. As an adult educator, I learned that this natural process had a name and was a skill which could be learnt and refined. We hope that all priests are taught these skills in initial training and continue to reflect theologically on everything they do; so why should the Church not do the same? The benefit of such critical reflection is that it helps us to understand God better, be more faithful Christians and relate practice to theology. In fact, Practical Theology has become a discipline in its own right and takes its place alongside other theological disciplines. At its best, it brings transformation and integration, it ensures that we do not exercise ministry indiscriminately, and that we do not allow the needs of the individual to overpower the proper needs of the institution and community. Review and theological reflection are about the Church and the community and not just the individual.

In essence, Practical Theology is about 'performing the faith':

> ... enabling the faithful performance of the gospel and ... exploring and taking seriously the complex dynamics of the human encounter with God ... It finds itself located within the uneasy

but critical tension between the script of revelation given to us in Christ and formulated historically within scripture, doctrine and tradition, and the continuing innovative performance of the gospel as it is embodied and enacted in the life and practices of the Church as they interact with the life and practices of the world.[5]

This is absolutely crucial to our thinking. Scripture and the Tradition must continue to inform all that we do and they, in turn, must engage in a dialectic with both the experience of the Church and of the world in order to transform our thinking. But it will not be a simple process since Practical Theology:

> ... offers fragments and themes that emerge from particular situations and contexts. It uses the language of themes and patterns, rather than systems and universal concepts ...[6]

A different insight into this process is the depiction of reflection as theological refraction which '... is required for the purposes of separation and illumination'. This is a process 'which divides "strands" and then reconfigures them into an image or an interpretation'.[7] Our work aimed to shed new light on review, to examine the individual filaments and colours in the hope of reconfiguring the spectrum into a more complete whole. Thus, as we considered texts and processes, we hoped that the emerging refracted 'themes and patterns' enlightened our provision of a theological rationale for review.[8]

Reflecting on Scripture

As part of my doctoral research, I invited clergy in the diocese to suggest texts which might have a bearing on Review and then considered a range of them in some detail. We focused especially on Exodus 18 and Revelation 2 and 3. Exodus 18 stands at the beginning of the Hebrew Scriptures, it centres on Moses, a crucial leader in the life of the Hebrew people and it expresses Moses' vulnerability and obedience. Revelation 2—3 stands at the end of the New Testament and relates to the community of the Church (rather than to an individual) and the shared responsibility for ministry and mission. In addition, the seven churches are distinct from one another and yet symbiotic; the behaviour of one influences the life of the others. The fact that we worship a Trinitarian God was also noted – a God in whom three persons are mutually affirming and accountable, subservient and yet complementary, incarnate and transcendent. A detailed study of the doctrine of the Trinity was beyond our scope but the image is compelling.

Emerging themes

From a study of several texts, three key themes emerged which helped us to root review in a theological foundation:

- vocation, response and obedience
- location, context and community
- the nature of the human condition.

Vocation, response, obedience

In short, Scripture confirms what experience teaches us – that vocation is a complex matter. It incorporates subjective, objective and divine elements and our motives are very mixed. Gideon hears the Lord speaking directly but needs practical proof, Samuel requires Eli's intervention to identify Samuel's vocation, and the disciples leave their nets and follow – apparently without a second thought. Nathan pulls David up short and identifies where he is failing in his vocation, Moses needs Jethro to help him delegate and prioritize, and Solomon seeks wisdom and understanding as he becomes king.

The disciples, like Gideon, discover that answering the call is sacrificial – though we do not pretend that being an incumbent in Guildford equates with fighting the Midianites. There are choices to be made in pursuing vocation – and the four Gospels give us different priorities for mission and discipleship; the Haustafel of Ephesians 5 emphasizes the need for relationships of equality out of reverence for Christ, and we learn from Paul, Timothy, Titus and Barnabas that teamwork does not always live up to expectations. From the Letter to the Hebrews, we are brought back to the need for faithfulness, mutual support and loyalty and encouraged not to forget the bigger picture of the Last Days.

The letters to the seven churches (Rev. 2—3) demand that we listen more, work together better – both with the community and with one another – and challenge the seductions of wealth, pluralism and disunity. The churches are told to remember the past and rediscover the love they have abandoned. In all cases, listening and sacrificial service are key, and obedience is not the optional extra it seems to have become now. The demands are both immediate and long-term and vocation must be worked out more than once as the context changes. Just as the first flush of romantic love must grow into maturity if the relationship is to survive, so the first excitement of being called by God must develop into a lasting lifestyle. This means that review needs to disturb the settled and comfortable, throw down gauntlets to the complacent and ask searching questions about the meaning and outworking of vocation.

Location, context and community

Location in Scripture is extremely significant; nothing is coincidental. So Elijah is found in the wilderness when he is in the depths of despair, Eli is sitting by the temple door when he meets Hannah, Jethro goes to find Moses in his workplace. There may be something to learn about the importance of place – in relation to where the reviewer and reviewee meet (is it better to stand back and allow for the objectivity which can be achieved by meeting on neutral ground, or to meet in the parish – by the 'temple door'?).

But there are other contextual issues that influence all forms of ministry and these need to be understood by the reviewer – at least partially. Rural ministry throws up different issues from town centre ministry; the Church may understand 'parish' to be a geographical area over which it has rights and for which it has responsibilities but the communities who share the space will have quite different views. The context is important not only to work out how to engage in mission but also because understanding the environment is essential. Thus, issues of pluralism, syncretism, materialism and accommodation may have an influence on us just as they did in Asia (Rev. 2—3).

More personally, the nature of the previous incumbent – whether he or she was deemed to be the Archangel Gabriel or the devil incarnate – can throw a shadow on a new ministry for many years. Beyond that, the relationship between the particular church/parish in question with the wider community, with other churches and with the diocese are also pertinent. Although the seven communities are in different places (in an area not much bigger than a diocese), they are urged to recognize their mutual interdependence and the effect their behaviour has on the rest. We cannot conduct review in a vacuum as though the reviewee is the only important player.

The human condition

Evidence of the frailty of men and women is very clear in Scripture and we should not pretend otherwise. Most people are recognizable as real people with a network of relationships. These may prove to be life-giving or limiting but cannot be ignored. Every character has physical, emotional and spiritual needs and is prone to temptation. Failure is an ever-present risk.

Moses is a family man who gets exhausted, doesn't think strategically and has to learn to let go, Gideon lacks courage and obedience, Elijah suffers from depression, David commits adultery and murder, and Eli's sons go astray. Paul falls out with Timothy and Barnabas, the Hebrews community fails to worship together and the seven churches are challenged about idolatry, sexual misconduct, complacency, idol worship and greed – to name but a few. It's all a far cry from the harmonious working of the trinitarian God! And yet – God continued to work with and use women and men despite their frailty.

Our own clergy are no different. They suffer from stress, burnout, failure, sinfulness, temptation and sickness. The details may change down the centuries but the basic principles remain the same. The issues of holistic, healthy lifestyles and integrity of body, mind and spirit must be legitimate topics of conversation at review. Relationships and personality traits must be open to scrutiny if we believe that God calls whole people and wants them to move on in ministry.

And yet reviewers know that sometimes they only partially achieve what they set out to do. In our proper desire to be encouraging, the temptation is to avoid conflict or to dilute our comments, to collude with the avoidance of important issues and the projection of blame onto others. We are especially good at sidestepping personal issues such as weight, appearance or addiction and find it hard to challenge complacency or insularity.

Personal stories

As I look back over the last eight years, I cannot pretend that every clergyperson's ministry has been transformed out of all recognition because of the review process. Neither can I fit them neatly into the three themes (identified above) which impinge on all reviews to differing extents. A few reviews just come and go, the forms look very similar to last time and the conversation is predictable. An incumbent goes through the motions, the interview may seem perfunctory and the papers are filed away. He or she goes home and is glad to have it done with for another year or two. If the reviewee is not receptive, the referees not honest and the reviewer lacking in insight, then this is simply a waste of time and energy. But Scripture clearly teaches us that the people Israel, Jesus Christ, the Church and church leaders expect people to answer for themselves concerning their performance and behaviour. Scripture expects Christians (individually and collectively) to be called to account. For example, Nathan was not hesitant in speaking the truth as he received or saw it, Jethro was positively directive and Paul was rarely backwards in coming forwards. So why do we find it so difficult?

Some of these issues are demonstrated in these real (but adapted and made anonymous) personal stories.

Ted's primary focus for ministry was occasional offices (of which there were huge numbers). These he insisted on doing entirely by himself, from the first enquiry to the last post. He prepared individuals and couples, provided follow-up and gave the impression he would have made the wedding cake as well given half a chance. Needless to say, not much else got done, his team – such as it was – felt disabled and there was some dissatisfaction in the congregation. There were other factors – as there always are – but an attempt to encourage collaborative ministry or delegation and the suggestion that unlocking gifts in others could be fruitful – all fell on stony ground. Nothing seems to have changed.

Or consider Ivor who was depressed, grossly overweight, scruffy and presented an unattractive model of priestly ministry. The depression fed the lack of personal care and vice versa. Despite the valiant attempts of the reviewer and the offer of all kinds of support, small changes are made but none lasts for long.

In these two cases, all three of our themes came into play to different degrees. Both needed to reconsider their sense of vocation but this in itself is complicated. It is difficult to criticize a priest for providing good baptisms, weddings and funerals if this is what he sees as his vocation. Personal factors relating to the human condition could be easily identified in the case of Ivor and, for both, the issue of the effect on the community and congregation was crucial.

The review process is tough and complex, then. Competing needs of congregation, individual and wider community are hard to balance; and do personal issues require help, sympathy, counselling or tough talking? Nevertheless, despite these more negative examples, there is a wealth of evidence that review does contribute meaningfully to the organic life of ministerial growth and transition and that theological reflection can assist in this process.

Will's review could easily have been insignificant if it were not for some sensitive and probing questioning. In fact, his story is a good example of positive action being advised and taken before things became too difficult. It's quite possible that, without the review process, an uneasy situation might have deteriorated rapidly.

Will was an incumbent of a medium-sized parish for seven years, having moved in from another diocese. There were no major problems but, at review, it became clear that all was not well. As a result, Will was encouraged to attend a regional course involving a couple of weekends and an action learning set. Six months later, he had got a new job back in his home diocese. He had been helped to reconnect with his early sense of vocation, to establish why he and his family were struggling, and in which context his ministry would be most valuable. All three of the themes (vocation, context and human condition) came into play here.

For others, it's just a matter of inspiring confidence or giving encouragement – a Barnabas moment – and review presents a forum in which to do that.

Jess was an associate priest working in a large church. She was gifted, committed and appreciated by all in her parish – including her three male colleagues. However, other clergy had suggested that, as a woman, she should not be in a primary leadership role. In fact, one had even questioned her attendance at a conference for potential leaders. The experience of Ministry Review could not change what had been said but it could present a different view and give Jess confidence. With some help, she decided to apply for incumbency posts, got the first job she applied for and is doing well.

At times, review comes just in the nick of time.

Hattie was covering a vacancy in a large church, fulfilling a role for which she had not been trained. It was a miracle that she made it to the review meeting at all. She slumped in the chair dejectedly and the normal process was abandoned. Within ten minutes, she had been given permission (as if she needed it!) to go off duty, and within ten days she was on retreat (paid for by the diocese). If she had not kept the review appointment, the situation would certainly have dragged on until complete breakdown was unavoidable. Yet again, the three themes emerged but in different ways. Hattie's vocation was to be an assistant minister and not an incumbent; the effect of a strong team and the demands of a vocal congregation meant that context and community played an important part; and the frailty of the human condition was self-evident.

For many clergy – especially those in their first incumbencies – review is the first opportunity to discover that they are doing a really good job.

Kate had been in post for less than two years during which time she had been undermined by an older colleague who seemed to challenge or twist everything she said – in public and private. His retirement meant that she was just beginning to settle into her leadership role when she came for review. Referees all spoke, without exception, of the difference she had made, her vitality, energy and commitment. Kate became more assured that she was a good incumbent and this affirmation gave her confidence to move forward knowing that she was in the right place at the right time. She knew all that deep down but review was a timely aid. The human condition (though not her own), the context and vocation all emerged as key themes.

There are occasions when more robust discussions need to happen and we avoid them at our peril.

Lionel was having a hard time. So was his congregation. The references sought for the review demonstrated this in spades and gave the wardens, lay people and colleagues a formal opportunity to voice strong feelings. A disastrous review was a turning point in the very long and painful path to resolution. Lionel is now happy in a completely different context and the parish is moving forward with a new incumbent.

I am not suggesting that review is a panacea and these examples are not presented as 100% success stories but they have shown the potential of review to transform ministry and to help individuals move on – not necessarily literally but in attitude or understanding. In the majority of cases, there was at least some sense of movement and transition, and the enforced reflection, reading, listening and talking provided a pause in a safe space in the frantic life of ministry.

Final thoughts

Where is God in all this? Is it naïve to believe that we can look for signs of God's presence in an organized institutional process? Of course, Christians believe that Christ is the head of the Church – and it is the Church that provides the process, and that Christ is always present when they gather and meet in his name. We believe that the Spirit provides insights and prompts with words and feelings and helps us to read between the lines and listen with the third ear. But communication and relationships require commitment on both sides and so it is the responsibility of both reviewer and reviewee to be open to God's nudge, love and admonition. Review is about the individual person as well as the institution of the Church. It is about one priest's ministry – and the whole mission of God in which the Church shares. It is about learning how and when to make a transition and move on in ministry in the power of the Spirit.

Further reading

Archbishop's Council, Ministerial Development Review guidance (2010), see http://www.churchofengland.org/media/1216788/mdrguidance.pdf (accessed 11 October 2012).

Society of Mary and Martha, *Affirmation and Accountability*, London: Sheldon Press, 2002.

P. Moots, *Becoming Barnabas*, Washington DC: Alban Institute, 2004.

R. Greenwood, *Transforming Priesthood*, London: SPCK, 1994.

G. Guiver, *Priests in a People's Church*, London: SPCK, 2001.

M. Percy, *Clergy: The Origin of Species*, London: Continuum, 2006.

A. Redfern, *Ministry and Priesthood*, London: Darton, Longman & Todd, 1999.

A. Russell, *The Clerical Profession*, London: SPCK, 1984.
M. Torry, *Managing God's Business*, Aldershot: Ashgate Press, 2005.

Notes

1. Society of Mary and Martha, *Affirmation and Accountability*, London: Sheldon Press, 2002.

2. A requirement of the Regulations was that bishops were obliged to operate a Ministerial Development Review scheme.

3. Since *Affirmation and Accountability*, the Experiences of Ministry research project (see http://www.experiencesofministry.org) has suggested that clergy are not as stressed as we imagined, which is good news, but we still need to continue the work of affirmation.

4. See further http://www.churchofengland.org/clergy-office-holders/common-tenure.aspx (accessed 11 October 2012).

5. John Swinton and Harriet Mowatt, *Practical Theology and Qualitative Research Methods*, London: SCM Press, 2006, pp. 4–5.

6. Swinton and Mowatt, *Practical Theology*, p. 12.

7. Martyn Percy, *Clergy: The Origin of Species*, London: Continuum, 2006, p. 11.

8. This chapter provides a snapshot of the work we undertook. Besides the Scripture briefly discussed here we also considered texts from the Tradition of the Church, e.g. Benedict, Baxter and Simeon.

11

Moving On in the
'Mixed-Economy Church'

TIM LING

A couple of years ago I was asked to write an opinion piece for the *Church Times* on the future shape of ministry. I side-stepped the invitation to engage in futurology by reflecting on Scripture and on what I considered to be some constants in ministry: personal passions, contested role authority, and changing contexts. The particular focus for my reflection was Peter's ministry, including the events surrounding the meeting of the 'Jerusalem Council' (Acts 15). Reading reviews is always an education. I found that at least one of my readers had construed the piece as both 'mostly uncontroversial' and apparently revealing of 'the mind of church-officialdom', that is, a penchant for bureaucracy. By drawing an analogy between our 'mixed economy of church' and the earliest Church's wrestling with change I appeared to be doing something troubling, particularly when noting the presence of long discussions and the writing of documents authorizing ministry (15.23–29). One result of my reflection was to create a disturbance that in turn appeared to provoke some distancing behaviour. I ceased to be Tim and became an icon of 'church-officialdom', thus transferring the source of disturbance from the text to its mediator. I accept that I could be wrong in my reading of Acts 15. However, it is also my experience that we can be remarkably creative when it comes to disabling the force of Scripture, one classic manoeuvre being to 'expert the text'; for example, 'according to Dunn/Wright/Gooder what Luke was really saying was ...'. The premise of this chapter is hopefully uncontroversial in advocating the essential value of a patient attending to Scripture as we explore the meaning of current changes in ministry. In the following pages I am going to return to Jerusalem but this time with Paul. My aim is to use this episode as a lens through which we explore our understanding of change and our place in it as we move on in ministry. In addition, I want to advocate more generally the importance of Scripture as a theological resource – something that goes without saying and therefore occasionally needs saying: 'In the course of doing our work we leave our work. But in reading, teaching, and preaching the Scriptures it happens: we cease to listen to the Scriptures ...'[1] I do this with some trepidation. I fear that much of what I say will be obvious and that some will jar as I both unsettle assumptions, and no doubt make my own (especially as I sweep past contested academic positions). Nonetheless, by using this lens I hope to locate our 'mixed economy' in a much bigger story than the parochial interests of the Church of England by probing what it might mean for Paul and for us to revisit Jerusalem, to remember the 'poor' and to realize our poverty.

Revisiting Jerusalem

> So Paul and Barnabas were appointed, along with some other believers, to go up to Jerusalem to see the apostles and elders about this question. (Acts 15.2b)

We've been here before, haven't we? The feeling that you are going backwards and not forwards as you expected. Your call was absolutely clear. The testimony to the work of the Holy Spirit in your ministry unquestionable, and yet, seemingly constant questions about how, why, when, where we work together. Why Jerusalem? What's the 'question'? How do we make sense of what is going on? What's the 'mixed economy' and does it matter?

The Jerusalem Council

The community that hosted the Jerusalem 'Council' carries many of the hallmarks of a holiness movement or religious order. The form of its common life was characterized by a daily devotion to the apostles' teaching, fellowship, the breaking of bread and prayer (2.42), and mutual care (2.44). The latter is often passed over but there was a decidedly communal dimension to their life, clearly present in the receipt and distribution of property to those in need. Elders were appointed and carried out these responsibilities, apparently for a time under the leadership of James, the Lord's brother (Acts 12.17, 15.13ff; cf. Gal. 2.9 where James is one of the 'pillars' of the church). They were a culturally homogenous group of Judean Christians that found it difficult to integrate the needs of others such as the Hellenists (the Gentile Christians of Acts 6). The community's life does not map easily onto much of our life together, the parish church, diocesan office or deanery synod.[2] Nonetheless, regular governance from this 'centre' appears to have been accepted as a requisite for the well-being of the whole church. This community became the authoritative focal point for the Church, at least for the approximately 40 years it survived.

The question that Paul and Barnabas were taking to Jerusalem was: how can Judean and Gentile Christians be part of the same community of believers? Some Judean Christians had arrived in Antioch and were teaching that Gentiles should be admitted into the church in the usual manner in which proselytes were adopted into the Jewish community, by circumcision and obedience to the whole Mosiac law (Acts 15.1). However, outside Jerusalem it appears that these conditions were not being insisted upon (e.g. Peter and Cornelius, Acts 10.9ff.). The churches formed in Asia Minor, during Paul and Barnabas's missionary tour (Acts 13—14), included not only Jews but an even greater number of Gentiles, who were not required to be circumcised or otherwise observe the Mosaic law. It became necessary to clarify some theological and practical details of Gentile membership in the church.

In this context Paul and Barnabas go up to Jerusalem, the 'authoritative centre'. What might they have felt? While it may have been perceived as open in the early days before the departure of the Gentile Christians following the martyrdom of Stephen (Acts 8) they had reason to imagine that they would not be immediately welcome (e.g. Acts 21.20). Leaving behind an established ministry to meet up with people allegedly inherently hostile to that ministry probably did not look like an efficient use of resources. And yet, what we find in Acts 15 is an account of people trying to make sense. Paul and Barnabas are predominantly welcomed. The issue is clarified, considered and discussed at length. Testimony is given to the work of the Holy Spirit, people listen to each other and to Scripture, and a judgement is made by a recognized individual in a position of authority – James. Finally, action is taken, people chosen and sent with a letter of authorization.

The 'mixed-economy church'

And now? We have a 'mixed economy church', a phrase with which Archbishop Rowan sought to name the 'chaotic' reality of our church, that is, the diversity of our 'forms and rhythms of worshipping life'. While the phrase has its origins in his ministry in Wales it was introduced to the Church of England at his presidential address to General Synod in July 2003. In this address he also painted a picture of a parochial system that was both working 'remarkably well' and that in other contexts was 'simply not capable' of addressing the questions that were being asked of it. He spoke of the need for something new to grow out of, or alongside, such contexts, for example 'church planting'; indeed, that there was already an 'extraordinary amount' going on in terms of the creation of new styles of church life in both inherited forms and in Fresh Expressions. The challenge was to find out what God was doing and to join in – to engage in God's mission.

The question that many are still wrestling with, as did the Jerusalem church, is: can we live with this? To some extent we have little choice in the matter. The pressures on the parochial system are not going away. Annual clergy turnover of around 3% is expected to increase over the next decade, with 40% of the Church of England's stipendiary clergy retiring as the baby-boomers leave the workforce. However, more fundamentally,

God remains faithful. He calls people into relationship, into community, by the power of the Spirit and in Christ. Spiritual and numerical growth is a present reality and significant contributions to the common good are made through the transformative presence of the Church. This is well documented and is often taking place in forms alongside the life of the institutional church.[3] This growth looks strangely familiar, as it should; after all, we hold to Scripture and sacraments as the essential common language God has given. Nonetheless, innovations in worship and communal practices often feel alien and occasionally offend our cultural sensibilities. We may find ourselves asking in these contexts: do we actually like the 'growth' that we see?[4]

Perhaps we can see ourselves among the various protagonists in Acts 15 as they seek not simply to live together but to be faithful witnesses to the gospel. In *The Future of the Parish System* Archbishop Rowan, reflecting on our responsibilities as we seek in our common life to discover more of the character of God, as it is lived out in Jesus, writes: 'The deepest theological resource for thinking about the Church now is this complex event which is laid out in the New Testament – an event which is in some sense going on now. It is going on now because the encounter is the same.'[5] This is very much a time for wrestling with this 'theological resource'. The House of Bishops and the Archbishops' Council have set out the challenge: 'to re-shape or reimagine the Church's ministry for the century coming, so as to make sure that there is a growing and sustainable Christian witness in every local community'.[6] In the shadow of the Jerusalem Council how did Paul re-shape, or re-member, his ministry?

Remembering the poor

> They agreed that we should go to the Gentiles, and they to the circumcised. All they asked was that we should continue to remember the poor, the very thing I had been eager to do all along. (Gal. 2.9b–10)[7]

When Paul remembers Jerusalem it appears that his instructions were clear and yet his actions tell us something more. The focus of his ministry is apparently on the uncircumcised and yet his practice may fairly be characterized as being first to the Jews. In addition, it is about both preaching the gospel (2.7) and remembering the poor (2.10). Indeed, the collection for the poor appears to be really important for Paul but its significance is less than clear. Is it about a preferential option for the poor that may be generalized or is it about a geographically and historically defined community, Jerusalem? Does Paul's practice give us any insight and how does his, and our, remembering inform our present?

Paul's remembrance

Paul tells his Galatian readers that he visited Jerusalem in response to a 'revelation', and 'in order to make sure that I was not running or had not run in vain' (2.2). Paul is being pretty candid about his motivations. His gift of insight, his revelation, has not overcome an anxiety to make sure that he was on the right track. In looking for certainty he seeks out the 'acknowledged leaders' (lit. 'those with a reputation'), an approach that appears to be full of ambivalence: 'what they actually were makes no difference to me' (2.6). Nonetheless, he remembers the visit, its importance for his ministry and that they addressed his question. He is affirmed. The grace given to him is recognized, the right hand of fellowship offered, and his task, preaching to the Gentiles, acknowledged (2.7f.; cf. Acts 15). And yet, Paul's practice is repeatedly 'first to the Jews' (Rom. 1.16, cf. Acts 14.1; 17.1, 10, 17; 18.4, 19, 26; 19.8).[8] Revelation and anxiety, leaders and ambivalence, espoused theory and practice, things aren't always clear.

What does appear to be clear throughout Paul's letters is his remembrance of the 'poor'. He's anxious about the acceptability of his collection and he risks everything to deliver it personally, a risk that results in the end of his public ministry (Rom. 15.26; Gal. 2.10; 1 Cor. 16.1f. and 2 Cor. 8—9). But who are these 'poor'? It isn't as obvious as it may at first seem. First, contemporary debates about relative and absolute poverty parallel discussions about the *penes* and the *ptochos* of the ancient world.[9] It is striking that the poor of the New Testament are overwhelmingly *ptochos* (lit. beggar), language that resonates with the designation of the faithful in Deutro-Isaiah, the remnant of 'pious poor'. Second, even if we accept 'the poor' as a form of economic designation for the destitute, it is not clear whether their remembrance is a universally applicable ethical injunction or limited to 'the poor among the saints in Jerusalem' (Rom. 15.26). The picture is further complicated by apparent references to a collection for the 'saints' in 2 Cor. 9.1; are they synonymous with the 'poor'?

Paul's actual practice points to something more than economics. First, there appears to be Christological underpinning to his identification with and concern for the 'poor'. He commends himself as 'poor (*ptochoi)*, yet making many rich; having nothing, and yet possessing everything' (2 Cor. 6.2). He also parallels the Macedonians giving out of their *ptocheia* (8.2) with Jesus's own 'poverty' (8.9). Paul not only seeks 'freedom from worldly concerns' (1 Cor. 7.28–35; 8.1–13) but also declines financial support enduring 'all things so that we will cause no hindrance to the gospel of Christ' (1 Cor. 9.12, 15–19; cf. 2 Cor. 11.7–15 and 12.13–18). Second, this is 'poverty' for the gospel's sake, patterned on the life of Jesus (Matt. 6.19–34; 13.22), and most probably a characteristic of the earliest Jerusalem church where care for the destitute widows and orphans are about sharing in God's kingdom (James 1.27—2.5// Acts 2.44f.). There appears to be an eschatological dimension not only in terms of the active witness to the coming of the kingdom of God in the present but of the eschatological pilgrimage of the nations to Jerusalem (Isa. 66.19–23; cf. Rom. 11.25; 15.16).[10] Third, he appears to conceive of the collection in terms of an exchange of gifts, material for spiritual blessings (Rom. 15.27). This perhaps provides the best explanation for his anxiety about its acceptability (for me the greatest challenge to the purely economic reading). The giving and receiving of blessings implies a relationship, legitimating his ministry.

Receiving the 'poor'

While Paul's remembrance may challenge us to reflect on our own poverty, our concern for the poor, and the quality of our life together, our reception of these traditions has often been coloured by contextual factors. The sacking of Jerusalem in AD 70 casts a long shadow over the eschatological pilgrimage of the Gentile nations. The early Christian communities required apologetics that helped them to communicate to Gentile audiences the shocking revelation of a God who was not only close to the poor but who even lived a life of poverty.[11] Ultimately, these communities became the Imperial Church, Christendom. Bruce Longenecker[12] helpfully narrates the story of how until the early fourth century our sources reflecting on Galatians 2 advocated a generalized preferential option for the poor framed in terms of the law of the Creator, who cherished the poor and needy (e.g. Tertullian, *Adversus Marcionem*). Later in the fourth century, while the care for the poor remained as a maxim on the Christian life (e.g. Athanasius, *Historia Arianorum*), Galatians 2 started to be read as referring to a specific geographical community, allegedly in response to Epiphanius's suggestion that the Ebionites, 'Poor ones', claimed to be the inheritors of the name of the early Jerusalem community (*Panarion* 30.17). The impoverished mother Church becomes a recipient of acts of charity (e.g. Chrysostom, *Homiliae in epistulam ad Galatas commentaries*). What becomes progressively lost, as the poor become objects of our charity, is our understanding of our own poverty and its implications for our life together.

We continue to make choices about our readings of the 'poor', often through the lens of contemporary New Testament scholarship, which holds a consensus that the term 'poor' was in circulation in the mid-first century and designated certain people who lived in Jerusalem and Judea. In this context Paul's reference to the 'poor' in Galatians 2 is clearly a reference to a specific group who are recipients of alms; that is, as objects of charity. While a consensus exists it is also challenged, principally due to the absence of early patristic sources to support this view. The argument runs that if later readings are dependent upon an allegedly 'historically illegitimate view' promulgated by Epiphanius (in the second half of the fourth century) then why should we unnecessarily restrict our readings. It continues by suggesting that it would have been in the rhetorical interests of earlier writers to make the connection. If it had been known, it would have been used. This reasoning serves well a desire to recover an economic dimension to Paul's

Gospel by highlighting the broader applicability of the injunction to 'remember the poor' – something that many patristic writers still managed to achieve without the need to abandon the scandalous historical specificity (e.g. Chrysostom's *Homiliae in epistulam ad Philippenses*)! Nonetheless, the appeal to go back to the earlier sources before the taint of Epiphanius, as if the early patristic sources were somehow contextually untainted, is strong. Indeed, I would argue that we may as well travel one step further back to Paul's letters and his practices in the context of contemporary patterns of piety of poverty.[13] His remembrance as we have seen is multivalent. It has no single fixed meaning, it is at once self-involved, contextual, and wrapped up in a story that transcends a particular community.

Ian Aveyard, in his chapter 'Growing into Responsibility', sets out what he sees to be the shape of much of our ministerial practice placing in opposition ministry as proclamation and ministry as a transforming presence. Ian paints with broad brush-strokes; nonetheless, ones that often reflect our reception of the significance of 'poverty' – with the 'poor' as passive recipients of our ministrations, rather than as pointers to Christ-like practices that require us to integrate proclamation and presence. There is a danger as we seek to articulate our institutional priorities that we implicitly replicate this unhelpful dichotomy, for example in our discussions of 'spiritual and numerical growth', and the 'common good'.[14] This was not the pattern of the Jerusalem church or the pattern of Paul. Whatever our other motivations and rhetorical interests, recognizing our own poverty, accepting the weaknesses of others and making these our own in imitation of Christ 'transforms us for our mission'.[15] It seems to me that by wrestling with the question of our reception of the 'poor' we are forced to confront some fundamental issues about our reception of Scripture and our practice of ministry. We cannot deny the ambiguities of Paul's ministry or imagine him uncompromised by institutional responsibilities and relationships.

Realizing our poverty

> ... sorrowful, yet always rejoicing; poor, yet making many rich; having nothing, and yet possessing everything. (2 Cor. 6.10)

Realizing our poverty challenges us to address our changing ministerial contexts and to consider how we are personally moving on in our mixed economy church. Revisiting Jerusalem we have started to explore the messy reality of living with difference both as a consequence of, and as a response to, our engagement with God's mission. In our 'Remembering the poor' we have touched on the use and limitations of such slogans, as rhetorical interests and ministerial practices change over time. 'Realizing' our poverty is not simply about understanding our current situation clearly but also about making real, bringing into reality, our understandings. It is about moving beyond an 'imagined (and sometimes imaginary) idealized identity'[16] to recover our true identities in Christ as the source of our being and practice.

Present understandings

When we reflect on our present 'chaotic' reality it is clear that in too many places there is a disconnection between our aspirations and our abilities to deliver (for example the inflated parish profile or the diocese's espoused support for pioneer ministry). Many of our structures remain simply not capable of addressing the questions being asked of them. The experience of ministry seems to jar with the narrative of a future marked by spiritual and numerical growth with a transformational Christian presence in every community, and yet, 'having nothing' ... we make imperfect responsible choices. Whilst we cannot return to the historical Jerusalem our metaphorical revisiting disabuses us of idealized notions of an authoritative centre dispensing certainty and comfort. Nonetheless, much like Paul we still look to centres of authority. We recognize 'pillars'. We enter into economic relationships. In doing so, we locate ourselves in a bigger narrative that includes both the cross and resurrection. Here we remember that in the dark ugly midst of reality hope emerges. We recognize that our efforts are not sufficient to bring about true healing, peace and justice, we live in the hope that God will bring about the ultimate transformation.

Earlier I described the nature of the Jerusalem church as something akin to a religious order and suggested that this might not be how we immediately think of our deanery synods, diocesan offices or parish churches. I suspect that it was the Jerusalem church's deep commitment to the gospel, to a common life and their concern for the poor that gave them authority, marked them out as leaders (those 'pillars' with a reputation), and made them commendable recipients of alms. The emergence over the last ten years in our 'mixed economy' of small communities that share these elements in their common life has been striking.[17] These communities resist easy labelling: area, messy, fresh, plant, parish, sodality, unit ... as they bear testimony to the work of the Spirit that blows wherever it pleases (John 3.8). We are perhaps too anxious to contain them, and the ministries they birth, with tidy classifications rather than learning to hear their questions for us about the nature of the 'centre', of authority, and of the appropriate distributions of economic resources. To whom do we turn when we think about our moving on in ministry, our ministry charge? When we consider our ongoing call? When we seek to check our course? Would you ask the local 'small community'? Would you consider it an efficient use of your time? How would you feel about being asked? What would the quality of the conversation be? What 'one thing' would you ask to be remembered?

Shaping our practice

When I write about 'Jerusalem' in these terms does it represent a responsible unpacking of Scripture or do my musings simply and subconsciously reveal the mind of church officialdom? What rhetorical interests are at play and how might attending to these enable or disable our encounter with God's word? Such interpretative questions have been wrestled with for centuries, as can be seen by tracing some of the history of how we have understood Paul's collection for the 'poor'. The discipline of such study potentially enables us to become more mindful, to rediscover lost identities, and to be stirred from idealized pasts. It also highlights the reality that every slogan, first- or twenty-first-century, has its uses and limitations. When we 'remember the poor' or 're-imagine ministry' we disclose something of ourselves, our contexts and the stories that shape us. We reveal our particular hopes and anxieties, the boundaries of our communities and the authorities that we privilege. In this heady mix Scripture has the power to disturb us and to contribute the framing of our imaginations and to be a formative influence. How might our 'moving on' be shaped by Scripture?

Wrestling with the accounts of Paul's return to Jerusalem brings into relief three principal challenges that speak powerfully into our mission context. The challenges are: to follow Christ, to witness actively to the coming of the kingdom of God in the present, and to collaborate. First, realizing our poverty, we follow Christ's example and, responding to his love, we are challenged in humility to regard others as better than ourselves (Phil. 2.3, cf. Mark 8.35). Whatever we may make of the rhetorical interests that lie behind Paul's self-disclosure we know that his return to Jerusalem was a risky enterprise that ended his public ministry. Second, remembering the poor, we witness actively to the coming of the kingdom of God which is not 'food and drink but righteousness and peace and joy in the Holy Spirit' (Rom. 14.17). Witnessing to this work involves telling (and listening to) stories about all the varied places where we see justice, peace and joy and laying claim to these as fruits of the Spirit. Third, as agents of God's mission of reconciliation we should be a living witness to the unity we confess (John 13.35). Paul's anxiety about his collection for Jerusalem and our incomplete understandings of its nature, and even of its reception, help us to locate our own stories of unity. These are both incomplete and bound up in a larger story. God's love does not end at the cross, our hope comes with the resurrection, and the unfolding of God's grace as we live together.

Moving on in the 'mixed-economy church'

I wonder whether we have ever not lived in a 'mixed economy'. God remains faithful. He calls people into relationship with him and with each other. By revisiting Jerusalem, remembering the 'poor' and realizing our poverty, I hope to have demonstrated how Scripture may feed our imaginations and provide a lively resource as we seek to move on in ministry. 'The Lord takes pleasure in those who fear him, in those who hope in his steadfast love' (Ps. 147.11).

Notes

1. Eugene Peterson, *Working the Angles – The Shape of Pastoral Integrity*, Grand Rapids, MI: Eerdmans, 1987, p. 87.

2. Probably more 'sodal' than 'modal', see http://sheffieldcentreresearch. wordpress.com/2012/03/13/why-modality-and-sodality-thinking-is-vital-to-understand-future-church/ (accessed 8 November 2012).

3. E.g. GS 1870, *Fresh Expressions and Church Growth* and David Goodhew (ed.), *Church Growth in Britain – 1980 to the Present*, Farnham: Ashgate, 2012.

4. E.g. the discussion generated by the Church of England's Church Growth Research programme, see: http://www.churchgrowthresearch.org. uk/discussions/notice/is_the_word_growth_the_best_one_to_use (accessed 18 October 2012).

5. Steven Croft (ed.), *The Future of the Parish System – Shaping the Church of England for the Twenty-first Century*, London: Church House Publishing, 2006, p. 52.

6. See GS 1815, *Challenges for the New Quinquennium*: a report from the House of Bishops and the Archbishops' Council: http://www. churchofengland.org/media/1163101/gs%201815.pdf (accessed 23 August 2012).

7. I am making the assumption that the incident narrated by Paul in Gal. 2.1–10 is the same incident narrated by Luke in Acts 15. Mark Goodacre, Associate Professor of New Testament at Duke University, both sets out this (the majority opinion) and engages in the debate on his excellent blog at: http://ntweblog.blogspot.co.uk/2006/09/jerusalem-council-gal-2.1-10-acts-15.html (accessed 17 October 2012).

8. See further David Bosch, *Transforming Mission*, Maryknoll: Orbis Books, 1991, pp. 95 and 123ff.

9. http://www.poverty.org.uk/summary/social%20exclusion.shtml (accessed 17 October 2012) for example; cf. Gildas Hamel, *Poverty and*

Charity in Roman Palestine, California: University of California Press, 1990, pp. 167f.

10. For more on the potential eschatological significance of the collection, see Bosch, *Transforming Mission*, pp. 146ff.

11. Hamel, *Poverty and Charity*, pp. 222f.

12. This discussion is necessarily restricted in its scope. For those interested in the academic debate and following up the patristic sources cited see further Bruce Longenecker's demanding and important text: *Remember the Poor*, Grand Rapids MI: Eerdmans, 2010, esp. pp. 159ff.

13. Tim Ling, *The Judaean Poor and the Fourth Gospel*, Cambridge: Cambridge University Press, 2006, pp. 62ff.

14. See GS 1815, *Challenges for the New Quinquennium*.

15. Fr Christian Chessel, 'In My Weakness, I Find My Strength', quoted in Chapter 5, p. 74 above.

16. Amanda Bloor in 'Putting on Priesthood', Chapter 2 above; cf. Stuart Burns on the search for idealized stable states in 'Creating Critical Conversations', in Tim Ling and Lesley Bentley (eds), *Developing Faithful Ministers*, London: SCM Press, 2012, p. 83.

17. For a recent description of small communities seeking to follow Christ and transform their communities (often working in areas of poverty and deprivation) see Johnny Baker's blog: http://jonnybaker.blogs.com/jonnybaker/ 'missional communities – something's going on!' (accessed 9 November 2012).